PERFECTSHUN

to be Human

© TeeJay Dowe

PERFECTSHUN

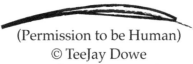

(Permission to be Human)
© TeeJay Dowe

Cover Design;
Ces Loftus : Creative Designer

Book Typesetting;
Jay Loftus : Pre-Press, Technical

First published in 2011;
Ecademy Press
48 St Vincent Drive,
St Albans, Herts,
AL1 5SJ
www.ecademy-press.com

ISBN: 978-1-907722-22-6

Printed and bound;
Lightning Source in the UK and USA

Acknowledgements

From the moment that I mentioned to the world that I was writing a book, a steady stream of loyal and enthusiastic supporters appeared and have continued to form a huge circle of cheerleaders around me. It has been so incredible to watch the seed of an idea germinate and flourish and finally grow into a whole book! The encouragement and positive responses that I have had from people as I have talked about the concept of the book has been such a confirmation that not only is it right to write it but the right time to write this book, too.

Thank you especially to Mindy Gibbins-Klein for coaching me through the whole process from concept to creation, it has all come together so smoothly and most enjoyably because of you.

For supporting me, cheering me on, checking in on my progress and believing in my work, thank you to Fleur McNeil, Susie Golics, Kiz Davis, Ian Gunyon, Glenn Bridges, the Inner Flame team, Tayshan Dowe, everyone in the SRI London Momentum Group especially the A-Team – Fleur, Amanda, Lindsay and Tasneem, to all of my friends, family, clients and fellow networkers who have already ordered their signed copies! I love you.

Finally an enormous thank you to all those people who have touched my life in a way that has left its mark – a lesson, a blessing, an inspiration and truth when I have needed it most. Thank you for allowing me to give myself

Permission to be Human!

Contents

Chapter 6:
Take Your Foot Off the Gas if You Want to Go Further!

Chapter 7:
Modeling (Without the Airbrushing!)

Chapter 8:

Allow Others to be Human, Too!

Chapter 8:
Allow Others to be Human, Too!

Introduction

The reason for writing this book is because in my work as a coach and trainer I see so many people beating themselves up, putting themselves down and making themselves feel bad because they are trying to be perfect.

They constantly bash their own confidence, belittle their worth and lower their own self-esteem - all in the name of perfection.

Hello!
As far as the human being is concerned - perfect is not possible!

And thank goodness for that, as otherwise we would all be finished, complete, nothing left to learn, nothing left to create, nothing left to explore, nothing left to aim for.

That would be a depressing and scary thought and yet so many people claim to want perfection! How many times do you hear the phrase "I'm a perfectionist" or "I won't be happy till it's perfect"?

I love that we are not perfect.

Not being perfect is what makes us individual, special, HUMAN! It's what makes life interesting, challenging, varied and exciting.

It's the very thing that makes you You!

It's time, now, to stop beating yourself up for something that is not even possible to achieve and instead celebrate being human and embrace all that that means. Set your own standards, discover or re-discover your emotions and be the most Amazing person you can be. No more beatings, just lessons that lead to Blessings.

Being perfect won't make you more loveable - you are that already.

Being perfect won't make you worthy - you are that, right now.

Being perfect won't make you better you are already magnificent!

The only thing you need to do is to be the best human being you can possibly be.

Give yourself Permission to be Human!

"People throw away what they could have by insisting on perfection, which they cannot have, and looking for it where they will never find it"
Edith Schaeffer

Chapter 1
Perfect is Impossible!

What is perfect?

I guess I need to begin this book by gaining an understanding of what is Perfect? How do you define it? What does it actually mean?

I had a few thoughts of my own that I'll share as we go along and then in my need to make sure that you get the right information (did I feel the need to get it perfect for you)? I looked it up in the dictionary and this is what I found:

Perfect is ...
O   Lacking nothing essential to the whole; complete of its nature or kind.
O   Being without defect or blemish:
O   Completely correct or accurate; exact; precise

Here are my thoughts about those definitions.
O   Lacking nothing essential to the whole; complete of its nature or kind.

If you are either spiritual or have religious beliefs you might argue that perfect is possible in a human because we are all perfect creations. We are all of God and God is perfect, therefore we, too, must be perfect. Lacking nothing essential to the whole, I agree!

But do you really believe it?

Or, are you still seeking to become whole? To find that something that's lacking? Do you feel something is still missing? Do you accept and feel perfect? You wouldn't be striving to attain perfection if you really believed that you were already perfect, so I still maintain that perfect is not possible, at least not in our minds and beliefs anyway.

o Being without defect or blemish:
Oh my gosh! We have whole industries that have grown up specially to perpetuate our insecurities in this area of perfection that we'll talk about later in this chapter. Industries that make us feel less than in order to sell the illusion of perfection to us, giving us another thing to beat ourselves up about.

o Completely correct or accurate; exact; precise:
Now, I can manage correct, exact and precise on occasion. I'm getting better at doing it more often in some areas of my work but I'm definitely not all of those things all of the time, in all areas of my life! And I'm so glad that I'm not because often the lesson is in the mistake, the beauty is in the imperfection and the humor is in telling that story of when things didn't quite go the way you expected!

You might have a job that absolutely demands accuracy, exactness and precision, such as being an eye surgeon. Maybe you are a pharmacist where, if medication is not correct, accurate and precise, the consequences could be catastrophic for a patient receiving that medication. Or perhaps a lawyer who must make sure that all the i's are dotted and t's crossed in order for a case to be successful or a document to be legal.

Whilst it is absolutely necessary to minimize risk and to aim for correct or accurate, exact, precise and have systems in place to support that aim, the challenge is, when we are human and an error occurs, do we berate ourselves, feel guilty, become fearful of doing it wrong in the future, blow it all out of proportion or do we accept that we are also human, put our hand up and admit it, share the incident to get the learning, share the learning with others and then move on?

13

Perfection and Perfectionists

Perfection, then, must be the quality or state of being perfect or complete, so that nothing is lacking, everything is exact, precise and without blemish. It is complete in every way.

Goodness! I feel stressed and overwhelmed just thinking about the prospect of attempting to achieve all that! And yet, isn't that what we do to ourselves everyday as we attempt the impossible goal of perfect? We even give ourselves the title "Perfectionist" and say it with pride *"I'm a Perfectionist"* to make ourselves feel better before we beat ourselves up again!

Are you wearing this label too?

As I started to explore what perfection is and what it means I discovered that perfection and being a perfectionist mean different things to different people. This somewhat amused me, to think that even the definition of perfection is not perfect, and then I thought, "So how are we going to achieve it when we're not even really sure what it is and when it means different things to different people?"

So I did a little digging and asked some of those self proclaimed Perfectionists what does being a perfectionist mean to them?

Your definitions of Perfectionists

"A perfectionist won't accept the fact that few things in life are perfect, that there are always little flaws, and becomes obsessed by the little flaws, focuses on the 3% negative instead of the 97% positive. For instance, a woman who makes herself unhappy because she's, like, 2 pounds overweight, when everybody else thinks she has a fabulous body. Or the man who freaks out because there's a little scratch on the door handle of his $80,000 car instead of being happy he has an awesome car. That kind of thing. "

"A Perfectionist is someone who is held hostage by the need to have something perfect before they move on, a kind of obsessive compulsive thing. "

"A perfectionist is someone who keeps tweaking something until it is exactly right - you could say that I am one, my assignments for my diploma are all written but I won't submit them until I have tweaked them all so that they are just right."

"I was about to comment that perfectionism is an unhealthy obsession, but then I realized that I suffer from it myself in two particular areas (one of them is English grammar - I think in grammatical sentences). So maybe it's a question of being "perfectionistic" regarding certain aspects of one's behavior rather than being "a perfectionist."

*"I would describe it as having to create something **REAL** that is **EXACTLY** as you see it in your mind. Anything less and it's not perfect."*

"Perfect is a nice word that conjures up the best our imagination can create. If we believe something to be perfect then it is and so it shall be!"

"A perfectionist is a strong, determined and highly focused person who strives for excellence and gets disappointed when perfection isn't met"

"Perfection is in the eye of the beholder."

Join me in ditching perfection and replacing it with Excellence
As there are so many interpretations of the word perfectionist, I can't help but wonder if, because at some level we know we cannot attain perfection, we have softened the meaning, blurred the edges a little, put in a few compromises and in so doing confuse it now with excellence.

For me personally, I'm very happy to aim for excellence in whatever I do because I know that this is attainable and it doesn't have to be perfect to be excellent. It takes away the pressure of impossibility and replaces it with the excitement of having something I can celebrate when I get there! I like that. It feels so much better.

O What's **YOUR** definition of perfect?
For example: perfect is always being right, without fault, precise.

O What are **YOUR** beliefs about being perfect?
For example: it requires planning and preparation, attention to detail and organization.

O What are **YOUR** rules for being perfect?

For example: to be perfect I have to take my time, always be on time, be organized, neat and tidy, be in control of everything. It has to be immaculate in every detail.

O How does trying to be perfect make you feel?

For example: trying to be perfect makes me feel stressed, under pressure, and that other people are waiting for me to get something wrong.

O If you replace perfect with excellent how is this different for you?

Perfection is a Deception of the Ego

You are Amazing without ever having to be perfect.
Think about it.

YOU:

o Can brighten someone else's day just with your smile.

o Have the ability to think!

o Have the ability to feel.

o Have the ability to create.

o Can turn a thought in to a reality by taking action..

o Can communicate with others easily and effortlessly in the words you speak, the words you write, the pictures you draw and even in your body language.

o Have the most incredible ability to dream and imagine, to create other realities.

o You breathe without thinking about it, keep your heart beating without focusing on it, produce the chemicals that you need in your body, just when you need them.

o Have the ability to inspire others through your thoughts, words and actions.

Need I go on????

"Ego controls the perfectionist and requires recognition."

You don't need to be perfect to be unique, different, special and incredible in your own right. Perfection is just the deception of the ego. The ego is that part of us that likes to be in control, always wanting better, faster, more but nothing satisfies it, so we strive forever waiting to be enough – good enough, loved enough, worthy enough, beautiful enough, wealthy enough.

Deceiving us in to thinking that we need to attain perfection to ever be "*it.*" Denying us the opportunity to enjoy what we already have, appreciate what is around us and within us, to celebrate what we have already achieved in life.

But we live in a world of millions of people with low self esteem and lack of confidence, because the ego says we need to be more. More like the media say we should be, as we are constantly bombarded with unrealistic messages, images and expectations.

Advertisers prey on our insecurities and fuel the journey of the ego to attain perfection, by selling us the perfect smile, the perfect getaway, the perfect partner, the perfect car, the perfect pension, the perfect house, the perfect pet, the perfect deodorant, the perfect new diet plan, the perfect career, the perfect... On and on it goes as they make us feel bad then offer us their perfect solution to make us feel better again.

Magazines show images of the perfect bodies, both male and female, not pointing out, of course, that they have been touched up and air brushed and made to look artificially perfect. In our naivety we think it's real and that's how we should look, then beat ourselves up because we don't. They offer us cosmetic surgery so that, "You too can have a body like this," but it's emotionally and financially unattainable, so we continue to beat ourselves up for not having the perfect face, or the perfect figure.

For some that means another big bashing for the self esteem and confidence, for others a step further into eating disorders such as anorexia and bulimia.

And it's not just a girl thing either! Men also see unrealistic images of the perfect biceps, the wash board stomachs, the pert pecs and spend hours in the gym… or worse… turning to steroids… to get the perfect male body to impress with.

If you were to stop right now for a moment, put your hand over your heart, turn off the ego and it's craving and it's chitter chatter and instead, just breathe into your heart, allow it to go quiet inside as you take three more deep long breaths in to your heart, noticing your heart beat… that beat which keeps you alive… keeps you safe… keeps you strong…. and then ask your heart, "Do I need to be perfect? Do I need to constantly strive for all of these things?" Take a deep breath in and notice – what does it say? And as you let go of the breath and the ego, know that you are good enough already. How does that feel?

Do it right now, pause for a few moments as you do that exercise and then write down your thoughts and feelings below.

Aiming for perfection sets you up to fail

Does anyone in their right mind deliberately set themselves up to fail? Do you get up in the morning and say to yourself "Right! How can I make sure that I fail today? How can I make sure that I definitely cannot succeed and meet my goal?"

NO! It would be madness. And yet, as mad as it seems, you do just that every time you decide that nothing less than perfect will do. You may as well pack that punch right now because you know it's coming and yet you are surprised when it lands. Ouch! Another bad day, eh?

I remember my eldest daughter loved to draw and to write. She just loved to be creative and she would spend hours on a project or a drawing, carefully constructing it, lovingly putting it all together, engrossed for hours at a time. Adding little details here, colouring it in there, looking up a word in the dictionary or thesaurus to make it more interesting to read. Her drawing, writing or project would be fantastic and I would be looking at or reading it and feeling so proud of her.

If one thing went wrong, though, even one little tiny weeny thing, that was it! It would be ripped up, screwed up, thrown in the bin for not being perfect. Off she would go with a scathing comment to herself about how rubbish it was or how rubbish she was and you wouldn't be able to talk to her for hours until she'd calmed down about it.

It broke my heart to see a beautiful piece of work discarded over a minor glitch and even worse, yet another beating up of her self esteem and confidence through her own harsh judgment - a false belief that it wasn't good enough or she wasn't good enough, unless it was perfect.

On top of that, she would have to start again, all those hours wasted when excellence had already been achieved and an imperfection probably would have gone unnoticed anyway.

21

Perfection is an excuse to procrastinate

I was talking to a friend recently about this whole perfection thing and she said something that I'd been wondering about. She said:

> "In the past I have used trying to be perfect as an excuse for not actually finishing things"

And I got to thinking about how many times I've heard people say that they can't hand in that piece of work today because it's not perfect yet. Or you can't look at the painting because it's not perfect yet or I need more practice before you can see it, as it's not perfect yet. I'm not sure if we do this because we really want it to be perfect or because we are afraid of being judged and found lacking.

I do know that when you keep your gifts to yourself because you are afraid of other people's opinion, you deny them the gift of being able to share in your creation. You take away the opportunity for them to appreciate what you have done and for them to support, encourage and celebrate with you.

Equally, it can be a reason not to start something. Have you ever not done something because it isn't the perfect time? Couples who are waiting for the perfect time to have a baby, employees who are waiting for the perfect time to change jobs, budding entrepreneurs who are waiting for the perfect time to set up that business. Before you know it you wait too long and now it's too late. Oh well, if you never got started at least you didn't fail... did you?

Susan was 25 when she moved from Stafford to London to work for a national newspaper and she was so excited. It was not without its challenges, though, as her partner still lived in Stafford. Trying to have a long distance relationship was a bit tricky and they eventually broke up.

She started earning more and more each year and it became increasingly difficult to see how she could manage without that level of income. The mortgage she was paying with her new partner needed both salaries to make ends meet and so, even though she loved him and they had talked about having a baby together, it was just not feasible financially to contemplate one salary and maternity pay.

They had a great life style, good jobs, wonderful holidays, lots of friends and a fabulous social life. Even so, while she was having fun, she did not completely forget the fact that at some point she would really like a family, one day. She know that her mum had been 38 when she had had Susan so she assumed that time was on her side, no hurry.

Even in to her 30's Susan was living a crazy life that was no kind of preparation for motherhood. She would work from 3pm until midnight as a sub-editor at a well known national newspaper, then jump in a cab with chums to Ronnie Scott's Jazz Club, drink wine until 3am and get home at 3.30am. Next day, same again.

How would a child ever have fitted into that selfish world?

After her long-term relationship ended, she dated a few highly unsuitable men. And all the time she was working hard and partying, her fertile years were ticking away. Pregnancy was never convenient because she didn't have the right partner, she was working too hard and she did not have the right support network.

Then she met Jonathon, who is now her husband, and everything changed because she knew he was The One. He was calm, kind and a brilliant father. He introduced her to his lovely children, who were then aged 14, 22 and 25.

They clearly worshipped him and for the first time she realized she was ready to become a mother. Susan was 34. Jonathon pointed out that her shift patterns meant they would never see each other, so she took a day job where she didn't have to work weekends.

They agreed that children needed parents who are married, so they got married and started trying for a baby immediately, by which time Susan was 37 and still naively thinking she could have babies, no problem. Her Auntie Sophie had seven, didn't she? Why should she be any different?

Besides, ageing celebrity mothers were popping up in the papers all the time, first baby at 44 etc, and she was fooled into thinking the same could happen to her. No one told her that many older mothers give birth due to receiving donor eggs or sperm, even donor embryos from a younger woman, for goodness sakes!

What she didn't know until it was too late is that a woman's eggs are viable only for 25 years after she begins to menstruate, so by your mid-to-late-30s you are a virtual fossil in terms of fertility. In her words as she looked back, "Leave it much later than that and you might as well go out and buy a dog - or at least pick up the phone to social services to ask about adoption."

Nothing happened in the first six months but hey, she was only 37 - still had long hair and wore short skirts - she could wait. And besides, she was busy with work. After another few months passed without success the couple decided to visit the doctor and have some tests done. Tests showed she had chronic endometriosis - a condition that affects fertility - fibroids and blocked fallopian tubes. IVF was their only hope.

Just when she was becoming truly fearful that she would never get pregnant, at the third IVF attempt, she did.

Susan was 40, and it was a wonderful feeling. When that blue line appeared on the pregnancy test she started sobbing and Jonathon rushed into the bathroom to hug her, they were both so excited. Soon her skin began to glow, she was looking so wonderful and feeling so great that they started choosing names and went window shopping at all the big baby stores.

But the euphoria didn't last. Although she had been expecting twins, she lost them both on Millennium Eve, at 15 weeks. That night she sat watching friends dancing, laughing and drinking champagne and went to bed as miserable as she had ever been in her life. But they were not about to give up.

They tried IVF another three times with different consultants with no success. At the sixth attempt the doctor suggested using donor eggs, because Susan's were clearly not viable. So they went to Manchester, where she received the eggs of a 28-year-old in an egg-share arrangement. She produced 18, they took nine each and the eggs worked - for the 28 year old that is - she got twins and Susan got depressed. By now they had spent £25,000 on IVF, and were in so much debt that they just could not carry on.

The harrowing experience taught her that if you wait for the perfect time there isn't one and you could miss out on all important dreams in life. She thought she was putting off having a child for only a few years, but ended up putting it off forever. Susan never did have her own baby, she and Jonathon chose to adopt a child and love that little girl very much so it was a happy ending, just not the one she had dreamt of.

> "Imperfect action is better
> than perfect inaction!"
>
> *Harry Truman*

Imperfection is a gift!

A client of mine said it beautifully as we discussed the idea of being perfect, she said, "I don't want to be perfect - apart from the fact that I think perfect would be incredibly irritating to be around, if you were perfect, where would you go?"

Exactly! Being imperfect allows for so many more possibilities and variations of the human being. Imagine, if we were all perfect, well then we wouldn't have cause to notice how different and unique we all are. What a tragedy that would be. I love that we are all different; it's what makes conversation stimulating as you explore the reality of the other person and discover how similar and how diverse it is from your reality.

Conversations would be pretty short if we were all perfect because we wouldn't have anything to learn from each other and would we even be interested in getting to know that person if we are already perfect, anyway?

If they were perfect and you were not, well, as my client said above, that would be incredibly irritating. I'm sure you can think of someone in your life that at times you thought was perfect or they thought they were perfect and when they have a little stumble, a little hiccup, something happens to let you (and them) know that, actually, they're just human after all, it's such a relief isn't it? It feels so much better not to have to constantly live up to that image.

I began my working life as a student pharmacy technician working in the local hospital pharmacy. I worked in there for two years as a student technician and a further six years as a technician and senior technician before having the rather unexpected opportunity to go to university to do my pharmacy degree.

26

I say unexpected even though I loved my job, one day I realized that I didn't want to do it for ever and could not go any further up the career ladder without a degree. It was also unexpected because I didn't have the right qualifications to get in to university.

I didn't stay on at school and take A-levels and all of the pharmacy schools required a minimum of 3 A-levels. I did have my technician qualifications, though, and 8 years experience. When I applied to the universities to test the water, out of the blue, two of them offered me a place!

It was unexpected, also, because I was a single parent at that time. I had a 4 year old daughter, a mortgage to pay and now no job! The degree was very much full time so I had to resign from my job and move away to Birmingham to study and I knew that I had to give it my all. I had to succeed and get my degree to make sure that I could make a better life for my daughter and myself.

I worked hard (yes, and played hard – it was the opportunity of a lifetime for me!) and I got extra tuition in the areas I was least competent, to keep me on track. The first year was the toughest for me, being back in full time education after working for so long, being away from my daughter who went to live with my parents whilst I was away studying, having to go back to basic sciences but at a much higher level than I had previously studied.

At the end of the year came the end of year exams. I revised like a mad woman, as I had to pass them all in order to get into the second year and progress my dream. I revised so hard that I even revised in my sleep and I have vivid memories of dreaming about organic chemistry and drawing out molecular structures and formulae.

Some exams I flew through, others were more demanding but I felt I'd done OK. You kind of know if you did enough or not usually, don't you? The last exam, though, was my weakest subject and although I really had put a lot of revision hours in for this topic, the exam became my worst nightmare.

I remember sitting in the exam hall, reading the questions through before putting pen to paper. With each question my heart sank a little lower. I could not answer the majority of the paper especially the 3 essay questions that carried the highest marks. I sat and stared at them trying to compose myself, gather my thoughts from the void that now existed in my head, searching for a thought that might spark another and another, to gather momentum to answer the questions in front of me.

Alas – there were none! I felt so helpless in that moment. I did any little parts of it that I could, to at least show that I did do some revision but for the most part I was blank and so was my paper. After just 30 minutes I left the room in despair; there was no point sitting there for another 2 hours, I just needed to get out of that room. I sat in the reception area outside the hall and cried. I had let myself down; I had let my parents down and most of all I had let my daughter down. That hurt.

I sat there feeling like I had just been dealt the most unfair blow, given the heaviest weight in the world to carry and the biggest black cloud was right above me. You know the feeling when you just want the world to stop, so you can get off? And just as I thought it couldn't get any worse, out came the year tutor in search of the student who left the room so soon.

She came over and sat with me to ask what happened and between my sobs I managed to get out some words and then she said the most unexpected thing. "One day your daughter will thank you for failing this exam because she will no longer have to live in your shadow and live up to such high standards. She'll know that her mum was human after all."

Do you think I needed to hear that in that moment? No! Do you think I have appreciated the gift she gave me that day ever since? Absolutely! My failure was such a gift, a huge lesson and a massive motivator for the re-sit in the September!

During the summer I went back to work at the hospital to earn some money, to spend time with my beautiful daughter and to catch up with colleagues. I didn't do much socialising, though, as I spent each evening revising, working through previous exam papers etc. I had to pass this re-sit in order to go on with the rest of my degree.

The re-sit came around and I was so nervous. So much hinged on this one exam it was awful. I sat down in that silent hall looking at that paper wondering what it would be like when I opened it knowing that those questions held my future!

At last we were told to turn the papers over and begin. I hardly dared look! As I read through the paper before I began there was a mixture of, "Yay! I know that!" and, "Uh oh! I don't even understand that question." At least there were a good number of questions, this time, that I could answer or have a really good go at; I did my best and left feeling that I had a good chance of passing this time.

The two weeks that we had to wait to find out the results were the longest ever! When the envelope finally arrived I picked it up and stared at it for a long time before daring to open it and held my breath as I read the word PASSED! Phew! I was so elated and so relieved as now I could continue my degree and achieve my dream.

"The most valuable thing you can make is a mistake - you can't learn anything from being perfect."

Adam Osbourne

It is imperfection that stimulates learning and growth without which we would stagnate. "If we were perfect – where would we go?" I cannot imagine a world where there is no learning, no curiosity, no growth, no change, because it's done and perfect. That would be SO boring. Imperfection allows us to use our gifts of creativity and intellect to look for new ideas and possibilities. Sometimes the thing that we thought was imperfect for the job becomes perfect for something entirely different, giving an unexpected gift.

Dr. Spence Silver, an inventor working for the 3M Company went looking for a strong bonding adhesive. To his surprise, by mixing simple organic molecules in an odd proportion during an experiment in 1968, he concocted a polymer that was exactly the opposite of what he intended to achieve. Instead of holding on to the objects after it was applied, the adhesive let go easily. In other words, it was glue that didn't stick very well.

Silver was fascinated by this rather than embarrassed and he shared his results with his co-workers. It's said that one of the many ideas that Silver first came up with was a bulletin board. A piece of cork board was smeared with a layer of his infamous non-stick adhesive, so that documents and photographs could be stuck on it without needing to use drawing pins. A great idea as you didn't put holes into pictures and letters any more but it never really took off.

Silver was sure that there was still a good use for his non-adhesive invention and he would hold meetings and seminars to share his invention and his ideas, in the hope that others might have better ideas about how it could be put to good use.

One of those many seminar attendees was Art Fry, a fellow 3M scientist who was stumped, like everyone else, by Silver's request. Art Fry was an avid church goer and enjoyed singing in the choir but was irritated that book marks fell out of the hymn books and he would lose his place.

He wondered if there was some way to secure the bookmark that wasn't permanent. If he could apply some of Dr Silver's adhesive on the scraps of paper, he could easily keep them in place and not worry about damaging his hymnal when they were removed.

The Post-It note was born and after more tweaking with the formula and negotiation with 3M. On April 6, 1980, the Post-It notepad was finally launched. As expected, it became a phenomenal success and gradually morphed into the many other products that abound today.

Imperfection allows questions that bring about improvement and diversity. When you take away the pressure of trying to be perfect, the answers you will find make the process of finding solutions so much more enjoyable.

Now you can create many options without worrying about the perfect one. Options bring choices that you may never have thought of or dismissed when looking for the perfect solution. Choices create movement and so you go from being stuck in the problem, thinking you have no way out to a variety of possible ways forward. It creates momentum.

David is an independent consultant and has worked for himself for 15 years. He has a degree in business studies and a higher degree in business and marketing. He works with large multi-national companies, marketing new products to launch into the market place or promoting current products in a different way.

David contacted me about 12 months ago to ask about coaching and how I worked as a coach. He had already had counseling and worked with two coaches but had not resolved a challenge that he was having that was affecting every area of his life.
He was depressed as a result and desperate to find a solution.

31

He travelled from London to Swindon, a two hour journey door to door and arrived at my office for his first coaching session looking very perplexed and anxious.

His first sentence after the pleasantries was this:

"I need you to give me a test.
I need to know that my brain works
properly and that I am intelligent."

WOW! The guy has two degrees, has successfully worked for himself for 15 years with the Big Boys in industry and he wanted to know whether his brain worked properly! I was not expecting that.

Of course I'm curious about why he would believe such a thing, to such an extent that it was dominating his thoughts and affecting his life. So I dug a bit deeper and discovered the reason he believed this was that when he sat in the briefing meeting for a new contract, he would find himself switching off, no longer interested in what the person speaking was saying, even though he was excited to be part of the project ahead.

So why was that? Why would he not be interested in the discussion? Then at the review meetings as the project progressed he would listen to the discussion and understand it but when asked a question such as, "So how do you think we could approach it differently?" his mind would go blank and he couldn't put an intelligent answer together quickly enough to respond in the moment. He noticed that other people though could respond immediately with very impressive answers.

The experience caused him to choose to feel inferior, stupid and embarrassed. And the more he felt that way, the more it kept happening. His conclusion – My brain doesn't work properly and I am not intelligent.

Noticing his language patterns (the words he used to describe the situation and the way in which he used his words) and body language, I had a good idea of what the cause of this was. I decided that I would give him a test - not the test he was expecting though, not an intelligence test or anything like that but a learning style preference test.

You see, as we receive information into our experience through our five senses – sight, sound, touch, smell and taste, we process it through a number of filters so that we can make sense of it and give it meaning. As we communicate these thoughts to ourselves and communicate them through speech to others, we use predominantly three main senses to represent the experiences - sight, sound and feeling.

We use all three of these styles but most people have one of the styles that they like to use the most. It's their preferred thinking or learning style. In Neuro Linguistic Programming (NLP) you'll hear it referred to as people communicate in an auditory, visual or kinesthetic (feeling) way.

Each preference type comes with its own set of clues, which are words, and behaviors that define how you like to receive information or learn and how you like to give information to others. The test confirmed my observations of David in that he preferred to communicate in a very visual way. He used words like picture, vision, imagine, seeing:

"I have a real vision for the project."

"When I work at home
I see a clear picture of the
roll-out to the public."

33

He spoke quickly when he needed to get it all off his chest and gesticulated like a mad man! All signs of a very visual communicator. As I explained the different communication styles to him and that the reason he could not answer quickly was that he couldn't turn the words others were speaking in to pictures quickly enough to have an instant answer for them, I saw a light bulb ping as he realized:

> "Ahhhh, so it's not that my brain doesn't work properly, it's just that it works differently!"

What a revelation AND relief. I watched the anxiety and frustration, the worry and the stress melt from David's face and leave his body, as he got the truth. We explored new strategies for him to stay present with all that talking and take notes as mind maps or charts, or pictures that he could see more easily and how to ask for the information in visual ways before attending the meetings.

And I celebrated with him as he turned that realization in to a strength, knowing that as he communicated differently, he added an extra dimension to the group, having the vision and imagination that his colleagues who preferred a more auditory way of communicating did not have. His perceived weakness just became his biggest asset. What a gift!

Stop aiming for perfection and instead look for the gifts, opportunities and possibilities that are hidden inside imperfection, just waiting to be discovered and developed, explored and exposed. Life becomes a very different experience when you see imperfect as a hidden treasure, rather than a failure.

So I invite you to join me in a new adventure as fellow treasure seeker and to share your discoveries with those around you, so that they might also see the gifts in what's not perfect. Give yourself and others permission to be wonderfully human.

What's currently not perfect in your life right now and how could that be a gift, opportunity or something to learn?

How could it give others a gift too? How can you share these gifts and what you have learned with those around you?

"The thing that is really hard, and really amazing, is giving up on being perfect and beginning the work of becoming yourself."
Anna Quindlen

Chapter 2
Permission to Feel ALL Emotions

Manage Your Emotions

You can't get far down the road of personal development without discovering a skill called "State Management," how to manage your emotions and stay in control all of the time. You discover that you get to choose how you feel, no one else can make you feel anything, it simply has to do with the meaning that you give to any situation that occurs. Choosing a better meaning means that you can choose a better emotion. A better emotion normally being a more positive emotion, of course.

The gift of State management

Being able to master your emotions and choose how you feel in a given moment or situation can be such a gift. It means that now you get the freedom to choose, rather than just reacting to an event when it happens. After all, an event is just an event, it has no emotion, it has no meaning but the meaning that you choose to give it; the meaning we give it, in turn, creates the emotion inside of you.

I can experience the same event as you do. We might both be there together to witness the occurrence and yet I might give it a completely different meaning to the one that you choose; therefore we experience totally different emotions. Same event, two meanings, two emotions. Neither of our realities is right or wrong, they are just different and neither of them truly reflect the reality of the actual event, they are just our interpretations.

The gift of knowing how to manage your emotions in any type of situation is that, when something happens and you find yourself attaching a negative meaning to it, and therefore feeling bad, you can reflect on that feeling and ask yourself, "What meaning did I just give that thing that happened?"

When you have your answer then you can ask a better question such as, "What else could this mean?" or, "Is it possible that it could mean X instead?" You may well find that this gives you a different meaning that gives you a more positive emotion.

Have you ever stewed on something all day, making yourself feel worse and worse about something only to find out that's not what the other person did or intended, after all? All that negative energy and time was wasted feeling bad over something that you assumed had happened - the meaning that you gave it - and it was all a mistake.

Stopping and asking, "What else could this mean?" would have given you the freedom to choose something else – at least until you could find out what really went on.

Stephen Covey gives a great example of this in his book, "The Seven Habits of Highly Effective People." He was travelling on the subway late at night when a man got on with his two sons. The sons were running all over the place, bothering the people and making a noise and the man did nothing about it, just let them continue. Stephen could finally stand it no longer and was irritated enough to ask the father why he didn't do something to control his kids. The father replied, "We just got back from the hospital where their mother died. I don't know how to handle it and I guess they don't either."

Suddenly you see everything very differently. They are the same kids yelling and screaming in the subway, the same father sitting there not noticing their behavior, but you look at them and understand them in a different way now and feel very differently about the situation.

What else could this mean? Great question if you want to feel differently about an event.

The State Management Trap

Understanding how to manage your emotions and knowing how to change from feeling bad to feeling fantastic in a matter of minutes is an incredible gift to have. However, it can also be a curse. I come across so many people who think that because they know how to manage their state, well then, they obviously must have to feel good all the time because they know that they get to choose, right?

They feel guilty about feeling bad because they should know better: they have the skills to change that emotion. Now they feel the pressure of only allowing themselves to feel positive - anything else isn't good enough. They battle with masking negative feelings with positive feelings and so begin to drive themselves crazy; now they are just flipping between the two states and beating themselves up about it.

Then there's the additional pressure of the people around you who, in your excitement about learning this new skill you shared it with them and they know you should know better. Now you not only have the turmoil of flipping between the positive and negative till it nearly drives you crazy – you have the added pressure of their judgment, too! Or, you're feeling that they are judging you. You hear their words in your head, whether they actually say them or not. "Pull yourself together! You have the skills to manage your state so do it!"

I remember talking to a lady named Jill at a business networking meeting. We'd got to know each other quite well, as the months went by; she was always bubbly and smiling, the perfect networker, mingling with all of the guests at the meeting and making sure everyone was taken care of. On the face of things she was someone that you would aspire to be like, successful, beautiful, cheerful and unflappable!

But I noticed that there was sadness in her eyes, if you looked carefully. Very well hidden but definitely there and I wondered about it but never asked.

One day she confided in me that this was a face she wore for the public and she felt bad that it was just a façade. The truth was that she was very depressed and had been for a long time. The fact that she had to put on a show, in some respects, gave her temporary relief from the depression but it also fuelled it as she beat herself up about being a fake.

Huh Hmmm...permission to be human!

There's a reason that you feel negative emotions sometimes; simply trying to mask them doesn't resolve them, it just perpetuates the agony of being unable to control them. Until you hear the gift they offer, they'll keep nagging away in the background, no matter how much to try to ignore them. In fact, denying them is downright dangerous.

The High's and the Low's are the Melody of Life!
All emotions are a gift. It's no mistake that there are so many and they were never intended to all be positive, otherwise we wouldn't have the so-called negative ones. Life's about balance isn't it? Being able to experience the whole range gives us contrast, variety and choice. It adds dimension to life's experiences, depth to our feelings; it's what makes us human. Life would be boring if we had the same note being played day after day, year after year.

If you had to listen to a singer who could only hit high notes it would soon have you craving for an occasional low note to break up the high pitch. If you could only listen to low notes it would be like a funeral march, very depressing. You need the variety, the contrast, the highs and the low's – that's what makes up the melody of life and the intensity of the feelings creates the symphony.

39

"You have to have the pain to appreciate the pleasure!"

It does not mean that there's anything wrong with us! We are not all suddenly bi-polar, we are just wonderfully human and it's time we celebrated that instead of medicating it!

Let's just stop for a minute. Think about the last week and list below all of the emotions that you have felt at some point during the week. Yes – ALL of them! There's only you looking so no need to hide any or deny any – they're all allowed on this page!

Excellent.
So, did you have a range? Did you have some balance there?

Go back and rate them on an intensity scale of 1 to 10. 1 = hardly there at all really, 10 = completely enveloped by it, totally took over me!

I'll explain why I asked you to do that in a few minutes. Save it – we'll come back to it.

Emotional Flat Liners

Emotional flat lining is such a common condition and one of the very worst in human existence. I have so been there and I wouldn't be surprised if at some time, if not now, you have, too. This happens really easily and from a place of good intent – you need to protect yourself sometimes. Here's how it often goes....

There are times in your life that you feel let down by someone, usually someone that you respect, trust and care about. How could they be so thoughtless? You can't understand why they would do that, you thought they cared and knew how important that thing was to you. You feel so disappointed, hurt and you resent it. You resent them for it. You'd never have done that to them. You won't ever let that happen again.

You start building a wall.

A barrier to protect you from people like that.

Then there's the time when you shared a secret with a so-called friend and they blabbed it to what felt like the whole world and you felt so humiliated. It just goes to show, you can't trust anyone can you? Next time you'll just keep it all to yourself. That won't happen again.

You put another brick in the wall.

Remember that person who said such awful, unfounded and hurtful things about you. How dare they! They don't know you. So rude. That won't happen again.

You put more bricks in the wall.

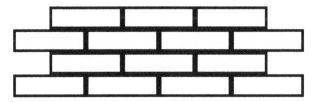

You took a chance and let someone you really cared about get close to you. It took a lot to do that and then they rejected you. It hurt like hell. You vow to yourself that you'll never allow yourself to be hurt like that again.

You put many bricks in the wall.

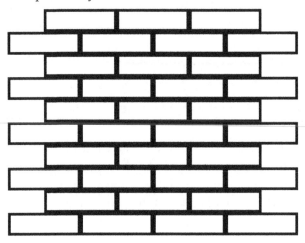

The wall is getting quite high now and strong. Protecting you from the hurts, the disappointments, the humiliation, the rejection. You live in your head, in logic and reason where it's much safer, much less painful. Switch off those damn emotions that feel so bad. You could feel quite angry, but you won't let yourself be that weak. You could feel sad but you won't allow any tears. Bury the bad emotions, ignore them, cover them up, turn them off. Put a lid on them so they can't get out.

The challenge is when you do that, not only do you suppress and dampen the negative emotions that you are attempting to avoid, you also dampen the positive emotions too. You can't switch off one without it affecting the other, they are part of the same – part of being human. You slip gradually in to emotional grey, fewer lows, fewer highs. The lows are under control now and so are the highs, barely a wave, you've had enough of the roller coaster. You slip into emotional flat line _____

Nothing to be excited about, nothing to be sad about, nothing to avoid or look forward to. Nothing. Just nothing.

That, my friend, is NOT living. That is existing. That is NOT how we are meant to live life. To experience life you have to feel it. Otherwise what's it all about? And beside that YOU deserve more than flat line! You deserve to live life to the full that means taking the wall down, DECIDING to be free and celebrating all the wealth of emotions that you were meant to feel, to know that you are truly ALIVE!

If you scored the last exercise at levels of 1's. 2's and 3's consistently – you need to take down your wall! Take out the emotional defibrillator and jump start your emotions! Do it right now... go on...put down this book, leap (yes I mean LEAP!) to your feet punch the air hard and SHOUT this is NOT who I am!! I am ALIVE and LOVING it!! I will celebrate the highs and the lows because that's what makes me human.

All emotions give you a gift
It's easy to appreciate that the positive emotions give you a gift. In fact, give you many gifts if you stop and think about it. The gift of joy and laughter is so freeing. The gift of passion that is so intense. The gift of enthusiasm that is contagious. The gifts of appreciation and gratitude that really connect you with now and how amazing life is.

The gift of love and connection with other people that allows us to expand our experience of life. The gift of peace that lets us know that we are safe and secure. The gift of excitement that vibrates through every cell of the body. Gifts of confidence, courage, sense of pride about who we are and what we have accomplished.

Here is a list of even more empowering emotions that you might also want to consider.....

Abundant	Blissful	Courageous	Euphoric
Accepted	Brave	Daring	Exceptional
Accomplished	Bright	Decisive	Excited
Achieving	Brilliant	Delighted	Exhilarated
Active	Calm	Dependable	Experienced
Admired	Capable	Desirable	Expressive
Adored	Captivated	Dignified	Exuberant
Affluent	Cared For	Discerning	Faith
Alert	Caring	Disciplined	Fantastic
Ambitious	Centered	Distinguished	Flexible
Amused	Certain	Dynamic	Flowing
Appreciated	Cheerful	Eager	Focused
Assertive	Cherished	Easy-going	Forgiven
Assured	Comfortable	Ecstatic	Fortified
At ease	Committed	Edified	Fortunate
Attentive	Compassionate	Efficient	Free
Attractive	Complete	Elated	Friendly
Authentic	Composed	Elegant	Fulfilled
Awake	Comprehending	Elevated	Gentle
Awesome	Confident	Empowered	Genuine
Balanced	Congruent	Encouraged	Gifted
Beautiful	Connected	Energetic	Glowing
Believing	Conscious	Energized	Good-natured
Blessed	Content	Enthusiastic	Graceful

Gracious	Loyal	Receptive	Stable
Gratified	Lucky	Recognized	Steadfast
Grounded	Magnetic	Redeemed	Strengthened
Growing	Marvelous	Regenerated	Strong
Happy	Masterful	Relaxed	Successful
Harmonious	Mature	Reliable	Supported
Healed	Mindful	Relieved	Sustained
Heroic	Motivated	Remembered	Tactful
Honest	Observant	Replenished	Teachable
Humble	Open Hearted	Respected	Tender
Humorous	Organized	Respectful	Thankful
Important	Outgoing	Responsive	Thoughtful
In control	Pampered	Restored	Thrilled
Included	Passionate	Revitalized	Tranquil
Independent	Patient	Rewarded	Trusting
Influential	Peaceful	Satisfied	Understanding
Inspired	Pleased	Secure	Understood
Intelligent	Popular	Selfless	Unhurried
Interested	Positive	Self Reliant	Unique
Invigorated	Powerful	Sensational	Unselfish
Invincible	Praised	Sensible	Valiant
Jovial	Precious	Sensitive	Valuable
Joyful	Present	Serene	Valued
Jubilant	Productive	Settled	Vital
Kind	Progressive	Sharing	Warm
Learning	Prosperous	Simple	Wealthy
Liberated	Protected	Skillful	Willing
Light	Purified	Soothed	Wise
Lighthearted	Purposeful	Spirited	Wonderful
Loved	Radiant	Splendid	Worthwhile
			Worthy

Pick three that you most cherish and love to feel, maybe you haven't felt them as intensely or as often as you would like to for a while. Write them down here.

When you have your three positive emotions find ten memories for each or as many as you can, times when you felt those feelings and go back to that time in the memory. As you remember the situation see it vividly, making the picture big and bright, hear what you were saying to yourself and what others were saying to you and notice any other sounds that were there and feel that feeling even more intensely.

Notice where it is in your body, what shape it is, what size it is and how it feels and expand it as you breathe deeply, allowing the feeling to grow as you enjoy those memories of it.

Wow! Did you know there were so many ways to feel good?? The amazing thing is that your mind does not know the difference between what is real and what is imagined or remembered vividly. Therefore as you remember all of those things and re-live them in your mind, your mind believes you are there, right now, and gives you the gifts of the emotions, right now, as intensely as you want to feel them. As that happens your brain thinks, "This is fantastic, I feel great!" and it begins releasing all of the feel good chemicals into the body at the same time, to boost your immune system and give you that sense of well being.

You are incredible; you can do that any time you choose to feel good. So choose to feel good often!

Negative emotions give you gifts too

Now, I know it might be hard to believe as you sit reading this right now but so called "negative emotions" also come bearing gifts. Think about it. We were given the ability to feel them for a reason, so that we can use them. They were made to be painful or uncomfortable or just unpleasant to make sure that you get the message quickly and move on! They form an integral part of our built in guidance system. Human emotional GPS!

A negative experience that creates the negative emotion can actually be a blessing in disguise. I totally believe that nothing bad ever happens to us, just things that feel bad at the time. Because at the time of the event we can't look back yet, we are unable to understand why it needed to happen, later we can see that it happened in order to make a shift in our thinking, or circumstances that would create an opportunity in the future. Holding true to that belief has certainly empowered me to get through some challenging situations in my own life and I know will serve me in the future too.

Back in my days working at the local hospital as a pharmacy technician, I was discovering who I was. I compensated for my painful shyness by being especially outgoing with friends I trusted and in the way that I expressed myself in the clothes I wore and the hairstyles I had. I was a bit of a rebel in that respect.

In my work, though, I was extremely conscientious and always held myself to the highest standards, I think more so than many, because I wanted to prove that you shouldn't judge people by how they looked but by the standards they delivered. I worked with some fabulous people and I got along with everyone in the department.

Everyone, that is, except the boss. Not my immediate boss, that relationship was fine, but THE boss, the boss of the whole pharmacy service across the local hospital cluster.

This boss took a dislike to me within the first few weeks of my being at the hospital, when she spotted me in the courtyard wearing a pair of boots that weren't outrageous but I suppose were quite trendy and fashionable and a little different to what most others might wear for work.

She made some comment that at the time I didn't really understand, I was new and didn't really know who she was, and it all went downhill from there! The comments about my appearance continued whenever she would visit the department and they later turned into threats. As I qualified as a technician I was told, in writing, that I could only have a job if I did not wear my striped dungarees under my lab coat.

When I wanted to continue my education to do a Higher National Diploma she put every obstacle in my way. At first I was not allowed; there was no point yet, because there were no senior technician positions available in the department. Then I was turned down because there was no funding, so I offered to pay for myself. Then I couldn't do it because they couldn't afford for me to be out of the department for a day and get cover for me. I offered to take a day less pay and pay for myself.

Finally when I pointed out the fact that other technicians had done the course with no jobs available yet, they didn't pay for themselves and did not take a day less pay or struggle to have their day covered by another team member and the word discrimination was mentioned, I was reluctantly allowed to do my HNC.

I was given the go ahead to do the course but she made it very clear, in private, of course, that she would never allow me to be promoted to Senior Technician in this hospital and asked me why I didn't just go and look for a job somewhere else? Ouch! That stung a bit but I casually replied, "Actually I quite like working here, I think I'll stay."

I managed to shrug it off for a long time; I'd grit my teeth and carry on. I'd put on a brave face at work and cry at home and look for other jobs but none were as interesting as the one I had. As it escalated I felt really bullied and began to get angry about it.

I was passed over for several senior positions that I was more than qualified for and had the most appropriate experience in, just as promised. The anger turned to determination and I well and truly dug my heels in get some sort of justice.

Eventually it got so bad that I finally got the unions involved for unfair treatment and discrimination. It was horrible and I hated having to do that but someone needed to make a stand. Who else would be treated like this otherwise? It took a while to go to meetings and hearings and collect evidence etc. but finally it was over and, in turn, I got the promotion I had waited a long time for.

I loved that job. I set up and ran a unit that was new to our pharmacy department; I was senior technician for cytotoxic reconstitution; I prepared cancer drugs for patients on the wards and visited the outpatient clinics. I worked very much in isolation due to the nature of the work but I loved the responsibility of it.

As I sat there working away by myself one day I remember thinking how blessed I was to finally have this job. Then another thought popped into my head out of nowhere and it said, "Yes but, what if you don't like it so much in 5 years time? What will you do then?"

Great question! What would I do then? I could go sideways, back in to the dispensaries, hmmm …been there done that….or I could go in to pharmacy stores, pushing a trolley around a windy warehouse, picking items off the shelves….that did not appeal, thank you! I knew I could go no further unless I had a degree.

Having fought for so long to get where I was, I had never looked beyond that but now I was there. I knew that I needed a "what next" to aim for. There's always got to be more, hasn't there, goals that keep us moving forward?

My battle was won and it was time to move on and use the determination that got me here to get me to the next level. I took that HNC that was so precious to me and applied to university to do my pharmacy degree. I got accepted against the odds and, of course, have never looked back!

A negative series of events that led to a life changing opportunity simply because I used my emotional resources. I am certain that had I got on well with that boss all those years ago I would probably still be there working away as a pharmacy technician instead of really making a difference in the community, impacting on the lives and wellbeing of hundreds of people, which is what I got to do next.

The gifts they offer
You see, you weren't given negative emotions as some kind of cruel joke by some higher power with a warped sense of humor, just to feel bad for no reason. Every emotion has a message and serves us, the challenge is that there's no manual to look them up in, no hand book that is given to you at birth to explain what the feeling actually is trying to tell you. Most people have never stopped and thought about it for long enough to figure it out the why.

"Negative emotions serve as a warning system to tell us that something is not right and we need to take some action."

Fear

You are anxious or worried about something that may happen in the future (near or far) and you start to play the movies in your mind about how that event will play out. Isn't it interesting how, more often than not, you run that movie over and over; each time you add to the plot turning it from an event into a disaster movie or a horror story filling your mind with all sorts of dread, blowing it out of all proportion and all you want to do now is run away and avoid the situation altogether?

Fear is not designed to paralyze you; it's designed to protect you. It is a sign that something is coming up that you need to prepare for, to ensure the best possible outcome, not the worst!

When you next catch yourself feeling afraid, anxious or worried about something, stop and ask yourself a few questions:

o   How can I be pro-active in solving that problem before it becomes my reality?

o   If I could choose to create a positive outcome for this "movie" how would I play it differently?

o   Is what I'm anxious or worried about within my control?

o   What would be five benefits to me if I did the thing I'm afraid of?

Hurt

When you are feeling hurt it is most often the result of someone doing or saying something that causes us to feel a loss, to feel less than or to feel judged and misunderstood. It is so easy to go into a spiral of self pity and victim mode when we feel hurt by others.

Often we have taken the action or words the wrong way and the person never intended to deliberately cause us to feel hurt. Sometimes it is deliberate and the other person just knows what buttons to press to send you spiraling into your insecurities!

I would offer these actions from this emotion before you allow it to take its grip on you and immobilize you.

o   What is the truth?
     Would that person really deliberately want to hurt you or could you have misunderstood them? As a mentor of mine, Steven Linder, would say, "Never let anything live in the world of the unspoken." You need to discover the real intention by asking them to help you to understand what happened.

For example "Yesterday you said xxxx and I took it to mean yyyy, I know that you would never intentionally hurt me and I wondered if you would help me to understand what you really meant?" This solution is elegant, it does not accuse them or make them wrong and it gives them an opportunity to help you – people love to help others!

o   What is your truth?
     Did you just give away your power? Is this who you really are – a victim? Less than? Someone who feels sorry for themselves? Or did you just temporarily forget in the moment how incredible you actually are. Recognize the lie and take back your control.

O   You carrying the hurt around makes no difference to the person you think hurt you. They cannot feel your pain, they have no idea of how you're feeling; feeling it even more for even longer still does not impact on them. The only person you destroy is you and you are worth way more than that!

So take the actions above to give yourself the freedom from this burden.

Anger

You live your life by a set of standards and values; you have, most likely unconsciously, drawn up a set of rules for yourself that must be met in order for you to feel that you, or someone around you, have achieved that standard or value.

The thing is though, you and I have different standards and value different things because we have different up-bringings. We may be from different cultures, we have different experiences and influences. We are different people.

Even within our own standards and values we have those that we believe are more important than others, those that must never be broken or violated and those which under certain circumstances it's OK to break or violate - we'll put up with it.

If I go against a standard or value that you have that isn't too high on your list, it may be OK to break that rule sometimes, you might feel mildly irritated. If, though, I break one of your rules for your highest value or standard then you are likely to have a more severe response such as strong anger or rage as a result - then I'd better run for cover!

The challenge is, though, they are just your rules. Maybe I didn't know what your rules are to know that I have violated them. My rules may be different and as far as I'm concerned I did nothing wrong and I certainly will not understand your anger over it. You might feel strongly about something that is not important to me. Neither is right, it's just different.

So the message is this:

o   Did I actually communicate my standards to this person or do I need to, so that they will know what my standards are and what I value?

o   Appreciate we are all different and that they may not have done anything wrong, in their reality.

o   Are my rules for meeting my standards too high for others to meet?

o   Am I expecting them to be perfect? Huh-hmmm... people have the right to be human and make mistakes, as do you.

Give yourself and others permission to be human.

Frustration

Frustration – that feeling that you get when you keep getting stuck on the same thing. It's that grrrrr inside that nags because you know there's a way; you keep trying things and yet you are still stuck, back to square one and it just isn't happening quickly enough!

Wow! What a gift frustration has to offer! Frustration says that there is a way, I just know that there is and I will find a way forward; it's just a matter of time and approach. Frustration gives you the opportunity to be creative, flexible, persistent and determined. What great muscles to exercise! It pushes boundaries and breaks through into new territory; it is the drive that will get you the outcome, as long as you learn to appreciate it and use it.

O   Get curious about what you can learn

O   Get excited about being creative and get in to flow

O   Build relationships by asking for support & advice from others and model those who have already achieved whatever it is that you are working towards.

Disappointment

What a horrible emotion this one is! That feeling of not getting something you really wanted or not being able to do something you really wanted to do, or the feeling of being let down by someone who either made a promise they couldn't keep or didn't deliver on an expectation that you had of them.

Here are a few questions to keep in mind when you feel disappointed in the future:

O   Did you have your expectations set too high?

O   May be they didn't know how important something was to you – perhaps you need to improve your communication going forward?

O   Did you read more in to the situation than was there?

O   Could you still have or do that thing in the future? If so – how can you ensure it happens next time?

Guilt

Feeling guilty usually means that we let ourselves down by not doing something we know we should have or doing something we know we should not have. In other words, you broke your own rules, didn't meet your own highest standards. It's a feeling that we can so easily get caught up in, instead of hearing and responding to the message.

That message is not one of 'you must punish yourself' – but that you need to take some action to make sure that it never happens again. It's not about seeking external forgiveness but forgiving yourself simply by taking the actions necessary to make sure that there's no next time.

Use the pain of the guilt to move you forward rather than making yourself feel less than or unworthy. When you know you have put steps in place to prevent a re-occurrence, leave the guilt behind – you were never meant to carry it around everywhere you go.

So what do you do?

o   Ask yourself "What standard that I hold dear did I violate?"

o   What can I do to be certain that I never allow that to happen again? How will I act differently in future?

Inferiority
That feeling of not being good enough, not worthy, not adequate or capable. You make yourself feel small, or looked down up on and feel inadequate. It's that feeling that makes you want to hide, disappear or become invisible.

The reality, of course, is that we are good enough, worthy, adequate and capable; we are just deleting the fabulous resources we have inside or setting ourselves unrealistic expectations that we could never live up to...would that be the perfectionist coming out again???

"So rather than use
the feeling to belittle yourself,
use it to go exploring!"

o   Have a look inside for the skills, abilities, traits and qualities that you have been ignoring whilst focusing on being less than.

o   List all of those things about you that make you equal, capable, able and good enough.

o   Note down all of the ways that you could improve on a skill or quality – what resources - courses, information or tools - would get you there?

o   There are mentors and role models all around you that you can speak with, get advice from, learn strategies from, be supported and encouraged by. List them, contact them and meet with them.

Stress

The feeling of stress can come in many forms – feeling overwhelmed, helpless, overloaded, uncertain. It's that feeling that happens when we are swamped by things that feel out of our control, over worked, too many demands, not enough time, not knowing what's going to happen to us or what's going to happen next; it's all too much, too big, we can't cope any more. You are out of control, don't know what to do, where to turn and can't deal with it.

The message – You are a wonderful human being who is attempting to be superhuman. Stop!

Take a step back and become an independent observer, a fly on the wall if you will and distance yourself from it just for a little while you will get a different view. You are feeling stressed because you took on too much and/or are making too many changes all at once and too fast. It's time to take back control in the following way:

O   Re-evaluate – look at all the things in your life and ask yourself, "What are the most important to me?" List them, go on, take a piece of paper and write them down.

O   Prioritize – decide which do I need to focus on most of all? Perhaps classify them:

    a. Urgent and important

    b. Important not urgent

    c Urgent and not important

    d. Not urgent and not important

O   Am I doing these things because they are important to me or to someone else? What is *my* priority?

O   Do I have to do it all myself – is there someone else who could do that for me, or part of it, so that the goal is achieved and it doesn't have to be me? People love to help out – you need to ask them though, they aren't mind readers!

O   Work through the priorities and celebrate when you complete each one. Realize that you are back in control and it feels good.

Loneliness

Loneliness, it's something we have all felt at some point in our lives, that need to feel connected to others, either with lots of people or with a special person, at various intensities, from feeling in rapport with someone to feeling loved, to having that next level of love i.e. intimacy with that special person.

When that connection is not there for some reason you miss it so much that you feel alone, apart and separated, in other words lonely. You can feel it when you are alone, especially if you are on your own a lot and you can also feel it when you are with others but you don't seem to have anything in common with them. You know the feeling "alone in a crowd?" It's a sense of not really belonging, or fitting in and it's uncomfortable, often awkward and yes, lonely.

The gift of that feeling of loneliness is a signal that you are a person who loves to connect with others and your need for connection is so great that it is telling you to take action by reaching out in some way to someone in your life. That could be to call a friend, text them, email them, pop round and see them or invite them over to you. When you think about it, it's nearly impossible in this day and age with all the technology we have to not be able to connect with someone at any time, in some way.

Maybe you have lots of friends to connect with and you would really love a more intimate relationship in your life, either with the partner you have or with the partner you just haven't met yet. Perhaps the message in this type of loneliness is that you need to take action to re-kindle the spark in your current relationship.

Yep, you need to take responsibility for the situation and do something about it by making time for your partner, maybe listening to him or her, spending time together away from the normal day to day stuff. Go on a date, do something fun together, look for all the things you can appreciate in that person and tell them, leave notes, voice mail, emails, little gifts. Bring back the romance.

Perhaps you haven't met that Mr. or Mrs. Right yet and you need to take some action, too. Make the decision that you do want someone in your life and start to make room for him or her. Decide who you want that person to be in advance:

What will they be like in their personality?

What kind of job will they do?

What education will they have?

Where will they live?

How will they dress?

What personality traits will they have?

What kind of hobbies must you have in common?

You decide!

Where will you need to go to meet this person?

Who will you need to become to meet this person?

What actions can you take right now to put out the right intentions to allow this person to discover you?

Loneliness was something that I used to really struggle with until I realized that feeling lonely simply meant that I love being with people. That I have a real connection with people because I really care about them and love to spend time with them. I find people so interesting and appreciate their different points of view and experiences, I learn so much when I'm with them and that I get the gift of sharing my interests and experiences with them, to allow them to expand and grow, too. Feeling lonely, now, for me, means that I really love being with people, I never realized that before and it's so easy to connect.

Those so called negative emotions, then, are all there to give you a gift, a message to move you forward. Learn from them rather than trying to ignore them or bury them, they just get bigger and heavier when you do that. It's like rubbish that we get – imagine if you put all the kitchen waste into the bin, all that smelly food stuff, and when the bin is full you take out the black bag, put in over your shoulder and take it everywhere with you.

It gets more rotten, it decays and it weighs you down, it gets in the way of relationships, work, goals, and affects your health. Would you ever really even consider it??? Never! So why would you do it with your emotional rubbish? Take it, feel it, learn from it, get the message, throw it out and move forward free from its burden.

If you're not sure what the message is - Ask!

There are times that you might not know what the emotion is, I know that sounds a bit odd but have you ever just had an uneasy feeling, a sort of dull ache in your gut that you can't really put a strong emotion to but it's definitely there and it feels unpleasant.

It kind of just nags away at you and takes the shine off the day. Like having a little black rain cloud above you and you're not sure why. I don't have a name for that feeling, either, but I have definitely experienced it on many occasions.

One thing I do know though is that every emotion, even one without a name, has a message and if you ask your unconscious mind (that part of us that runs the body without us having to think about it) a question, it has to give you an answer.

So go ahead and ask yourself, "What is the message in this feeling? What do I need to know or do?" The first few answers that you get are probably not the real answers. These answers are normally the answers from that little voice in your head – the conscious mind trying to work it out logically.

You will absolutely know when you get the right answer – that will be the answer from the voice in the heart – your unconscious mind, giving you the truth from your emotions. You will know it in your gut clear as day when you have the real answer.

I remember a few years ago deciding that the logical and sensible thing to do was to sell my house, move somewhere smaller and have a fresh start. It was the rational thing to do under the circumstances, I had ended my relationship and didn't need such a big house and it would help me financially, so of course it was the wise thing to do.

As the decision was made I got on with the planning and noticed that each day an uneasy feeling inside me grew. It was like a dull ache in the pit of my stomach and I had no clue why it was there.

There was nothing bad happening in my life, in fact, quite the opposite! I was really having an amazing time exploring who I was and what I wanted and choosing who I was going to become! And yet here I was with this 'bad feeling' about something and didn't know what.

Then I discovered that amazing fact – that you can just ask your mind and that it has no choice but to give you an answer! How cool is that? So I did. At first I got random answers that could have been right but they certainly didn't feel right because that feeling was still there.

So I persisted, asking over and over until Bingo! There it was! The answer. I know it as soon as I had it because that 'black' feeling instantly disappeared – Do not sell the house, it's the logical thing to do but it's not the right thing to do. Stay.

Oh my gosh! That was not the answer I had expected but it definitely was true and I realized that the feeling began soon after I made the decision to move and grew with every plan made. I felt SO much lighter just at the thought of now staying. That was it. I stayed put. A few years later, along came the decision to move once more, this time though it was under very different and much more positive circumstances and it felt so right. This time I moved.

You are more powerful than you will ever know. You have the ability to feel all the emotions, use them to your best advantage by allowing yourself to go there, get the message, take the action and get the blessing and if you're not sure – just ask! Your unconscious mind has to give you an answer.

"The feeling is often the deeper truth, the opinion the more superficial one."
~*Augustus William Hare and Julius Charles Hare,*
Guesses at Truth, by Two Brothers, 1827

Its's ok to feel down - Just don't live there!
For many people, avoiding the negative emotions is a way to protect themselves from the pain, and as we discussed a little earlier in this chapter the downside of that is you don't get to feel the pleasure either as you go into emotional grey. Other people avoid the negative emotions because they think they shouldn't go there and they fall into the "state management trap."

You know what?

It's OK to feel down - just don't live there!
Give yourself permission to be human!

63

During a presentation at a networking meeting, we were talking about the highs and the lows and the people who thought they had to manage their state every minute of every day. Afterwards, a gentleman said to me, "Thank you so much for saying that it was OK to feel down. I have been struggling with that for two years! There are times when I really just want and need to feel down, feel a bit sorry for myself, feel low but I feel the pressure of I should know better and what will other people think and so I just try to pick myself up and put a brave face on it and carry on and it's awful! Now, finally I understand that it's not only OK to go there but that I actually need to sometimes, not to wallow in the emotion but to get the lesson so I can move forward."

Exactly!

This is the story of life...
There we are, tootling along, everything is great and then out of the blue something happens that shakes us, knocks us off guard, takes away our certainty – yep, life happens and we feel shaky. If we feel too shaky we fall down the emotional slide to the depths of that emotion, it feels bad, we don't like it and sometimes we hit rock bottom.

The low is the pain we need to give us a proverbial kick up the ass! It feels bad for good reason – so we don't stay there too long! For some people, though, they go there, get some attention from it and then stay there for the attention and connection with others that it gives them. They feel more significant with the pain than without it, so they use it to meet their needs; they get stuck there because they didn't look for the lesson to help them to meet their needs in a more positive way.

That is not the intention of a negative emotion. It's not there to trap you but to propel you. Go there yes, don't live there - get the lesson that moves you forward to get the blessing that you deserve.

If at rock bottom, you feel you can't cope and off you go to the doctor you are likely to come back with a prescription for something that is supposed to make you feel better. The doctor is just doing his job, thinks he's doing the right thing, I can't knock that but think about it - the medication numbs the pain but it doesn't get you back to normal, it just helps you to exist.

If you numb the pain, how can the pain serve you? Numbing the pain actually has the opposite effect – it prolongs the pain because it's not quite so bad, so you don't get the lesson to get the blessing – you just hover above the bottom thinking it's better than it was so that's something. You will put up with the side effects if means you don't have to feel the pain, but the pain was meant to be temporary, now you are making it less intense but more pervasive.

You weren't meant to exist at, "It's not so bad," but to LIVE and feel that aliveness!

I'm not saying all medication is bad but I do think that our "quick fix" is often the long journey. I see people on medication long term who should never have been put on it in the first place and now believe that they need it to carry on. The GP advises you to keep taking it because they don't want to be responsible for what happens if you don't, not realizing that actually – you would probably be so much better off without it.

If you are currently taking medication for anxiety or depression I am NOT telling you to stop it. I am simply inviting you to consider taking back the control, discovering the truth about who you really are. Remember all the gifts that you have inside and to seek help to get the lessons, and advice to come off the medication as gradually as appropriate, so that you can live the life you are meant to have.

Perhaps the pain will give you the gift of discovering a limiting belief about yourself that has been holding you back.

Claire desperately wanted to lose weight, she didn't need to lose a lot, maybe about a stone or so, but try as she might it would just not shift. She was so unhappy about it and so frustrated that finally she plucked up the courage to speak with a coach about it. As the coach worked with her about why she wanted to lose weight, what was her ideal weight and picture of health she realized that when she thought of herself being that slim Claire, it caused a feeling in the pit of her stomach that was uneasy. What was that? She couldn't put words to it at first.

As the conversation continued and she began to allow new thoughts about her ideal weight to emerge, she suddenly realized that that feeling in her stomach was the result of a belief that she had about being slim. The belief took her by surprise because the belief was, "If I become slim I'll turn into the most disgusting, horrible and nasty person!"

How could that be? The coach asked her, "is that who you really are?" She said, "No of course not! I don't know where that's coming from!" And of course, if being slim meant becoming this disgusting, horrible and nasty person then no way could her unconscious mind allow her to be slim! Holding on to the weight as it had been doing was a protection mechanism, due to the belief.

As the session continued she got the breakthrough that she needed to move forward. She discovered that the belief went back to a relationship several years ago. The last time she was her ideal weight she lived with a man who abused her physically and mentally and would say the most awful things about her, so often that she had unconsciously taken them on as true never questioning them until now.

Of course, now that the belief that was holding her back and it's root cause had been exposed, the coach could work with her to eliminate it and replace it with a much more empowering belief about herself. Claire became her ideal weight within a matter of weeks!

Perhaps the pain will give you the gift of a creative breakthrough...

Brad is a working class lad, born in Manchester. He's had his fair share of adversity in his life, serious adversity at times. Even so, when I spoke with him a couple of days ago he told me that, as mad as it seems, he would not change any of it.

Certain events in his life in Manchester led to Brad having to leave his family and his home city and relocate. He found himself living in Somerset and having to make a new life himself. Actually tougher than that, he found himself working in London, renting digs there and having to maintain a home in Somerset at the same time.

Money was tight; he was literally living hand to mouth trying to make ends meet. The job was salaried and therefore "hours to get the job done," there was no overtime, as such, to boost the income but he was working up to 80 hours a week. Brad was broke, exhausted and stressed and beginning to resent it.

The tipping point for Brad came driving back to his digs on the A13 one night past all the big houses. He noticed a beautiful Jaguar pull in to one of the houses and watched as the huge electric gates parted to let its owner through. In that moment he realized that doing what he was doing, working for someone else, it didn't matter how hard he worked or how high he got up the ladder, he would still probably never be able to afford the gates let alone the house and car to go with them!

Brad concluded that to really make serious money, you need to work for yourself so he left his job in London and headed back to Somerset to start a business. Full of enthusiasm, flashes of brilliance and determination, he took control of his life and began his first business. And then...nothing. He was still broke but now the enthusiasm was waning and the safety net financially was gone.

There were no more coins down the back of the sofa; he'd long since found them and spent them. There were no plan B's, no choices left and he had a family to support. His wife had had enough of the worry and made it her mission to find him a job. He arrived home one day to discover she had seen an advert in a Pizza place in Burnham on Sea and was most definitely expecting Brad to apply.

He tried to object with, "I have my own business, we'll be rich one day," but it wasn't that day. Off he went to be interviewed and duly awarded the position of Pizza Delivery Boy. It sucked. He hated it. He was working his business in the week and delivering pizzas in the evenings and weekends. Out early each morning to go to business networking meetings and home late in the evenings after his pizza shifts.

Out one day he remembered that his mum always used to say, "It can always be worse...there's always someone in a worse position than you." As he resented that at first and then thought about it, a shift in psychology happened. It dawned on him that the reason he was delivering pizzas was to keep his family afloat, to provide for his wife and kids and instead of feeling resentment he felt a sense of pride in who he was. A sense of purpose took over and kept him going.

The final straw, the pivotal moment, the turning point in pain came one evening when out delivering pizzas. Brad pulled up at the house on his scooter with his pizza boxes in hand and knocked on the door as usual. This time though as the door opened he recognized the man of the house, it was a client, a man he had met a few weeks earlier and was doing some work with. In Brad's words he thought "Oh xxxx!" He was so embarrassed; if the world could have opened and swallowed anyone one up he would have wished it was him, in that moment.

He left the house vowing, "No More! I need to do something, something has got to change." He thought about what was it that was missing? Why was he struggling? Simple, he needed people, appointments, someone to bounce ideas off. Networking was supposed to be filling that need but a certain large and well known networking group had asked him to leave and the others weren't doing it for him.

So whilst he continued to deliver pizzas he used the time to plan in his pain, feeling those negative emotions, to do something, take action. If networking did not meet his needs he would create a new networking business that did! 4Networking was born. The old boys of networking said it wouldn't work but when your pain causes a shift in your creative genius, it's hard to fail!

Now just a few years on 4Networking is the UK's largest joined up network with over 250 linked groups who meet 4 days a week. A web forum that has 36,000 members and is not only creating discussions but business alongside that. And as I'm writing this the dream to be international is becoming reality as one of 4N's Directors flew to Australia a few days ago, to set groups up in Australia, New Zealand and Singapore.

Or maybe a shift in identity that inspires others...

Anthony had been so badly bullied at school that over the years he had almost every bone in his body broken, at times the same bone in several places. He had had his life threatened at knife point and on a number of occasions he truly believed that he was about to die at the hands of these terrible bullies.

He had told the teachers about it when it first started to happen but nothing was done. He had reported it again the next time but nothing was done. Soon he lost faith in the ability of the teachers to act or care, he was on his own. He felt confused. Why him? What had he done to deserve this? He felt truly helpless, worthless and utterly miserable.

When his parents would get suspicious and ask about the injuries, minor ones at first, he would make up excuses and stories. He couldn't tell them he was being bullied, he felt too ashamed and scared to tell them the truth. He even managed to convince them that the broken bones were due to other causes and somehow they believed him.

On the one hand, he was relieved not to tell them the truth and have to relive the experience as he recounted it, to watch them react, get angry, embarrass him by going to school or worse - to the kids parents and make it ten times worse for him. And on the other, he was building up a huge resentment – How could they not question it further? How could they not care enough to want to get to the bottom of it? They didn't love him!

It got so bad and he got so scared that at sixteen years old he found excuses, reasons to leave his parents and the school he was at in Ireland to go and live with his aunt and uncle in Swindon. His confidence was low, his self esteem almost non-existent and he was lonely, resentful, hurt and feeling worthless.

At the new college he made few friends as he came across as distant, stand-offish and unapproachable. In reality he was scared that if he let people in it would start again. So he kept his secret, that burden of being bullied almost to death quite literally, to himself, never speaking to anyone about it not even his family.

Then last summer he got the opportunity to attend a four day residential course run by a local charity called "Inner Flame" whose mission it is to inspire young people to reach their potential. He went to the taster day at the climbing wall and really enjoyed it and signed up for the course with a friend, in the hope that it would help him to find a way to re-build his life.

He was not disappointed! After a rocky start to the course and some very emotional moments, swinging between feeling involved and feeling totally alone finally, on day three, he hit rock bottom and confided in one of the coaches that he had had enough pain. It was time to deal with it and let it go.

The coaching that followed was very different as he was taken through a process to let go of anger, sadness, fear, hurt and guilt – all of those negative emotions that he had been carrying for so long and finally be free to go forward without them.

Phew!

The next day he was very different! With a new mission and a new found energy and a vision of no longer keeping it to himself, Anthony was able instead to use the experience to speak with other young people who have been bullied, to give them hope. To show them that no matter what they go through they can still get help, still get through and make a difference. Be able to give people the message that you are worthy, it is not your fault, you are amazing.

A shift in perspective that, as horrific as it was, to be bullied in such a way, was for a reason, to serve a higher purpose. Now, with a shift in identity from victim to hero, Anthony is helping other bully victims to get through their own ordeals and to come out stronger and proud of who they are. No longer the victim, afraid or feeling weak but empowered and able to choose who they become.

After the course he returned to college and began to make some changes in the way he interacted with teachers and pupils alike. He opened up, started to volunteer to help out with projects and gave so much more of himself that every one noticed. By the end of the term he had grown into this new identity so much that the college honored him with a gift of £100 to spend on himself. He was both surprised and thrilled and it was so well deserved.

Think back into your past – List three events that caused you pain at the time but have since turned out to bring you blessings? Those events that you couldn't make sense of at the time but without that thing happening you would not have gone on to do something you're now really proud of? What was the event, what was the pain and what was the blessing? Write them in the spaces below:

1.

2.

3.

"Let's not forget that
the little emotions are the
great captains of our lives and
we obey them without realizing it."
Vincent Van Gogh, 1889

Chapter 3
Self Development is about being a Better Person, Not a Perfect Person!

"Certain flaws are
necessary for the whole.
It would seem strange if
old friends lacked certain quirks."

Goethe

Imperfection leaves room for improvement

The joy of being human is that there is always room for improvement: something to learn, something new to experience, a new problem to solve and a new opportunity to improve on something we already have or do. It's what keeps us alive, excited and growing. Imagine being perfect and having everything, being everything, done everything - it's all perfect...And probably very boring, too, now there's nothing left to aim for, inspire you or challenge you.

If the truth be known, we actually do love the thrill of the challenges and the excitement of the possibility of pushing our boundaries and achieving new things, having a go at something, whether you're great at it or not, because you want to have the experience, not to be perfect at it. That's a very different feeling to the one we put ourselves under, trying to be perfect at everything.

Self Development is not a competitive sport

Often what starts out to be a journey of self development turns in to a journey of perfection somewhere along the way, as you discover other people doing and being so much more than you are. You want what they've got physically, emotionally, in qualifications, maybe, or wealth, business, relationships or all of those things! You want it all and more. You want to be perfect in every area of your life.

Now, there is absolutely nothing wrong with wanting to be better in every area of life; that's why we set balanced goals to support us in achieving that aim. It's the people who turn self development in to a competitive sport that worry me!

If you have been to any self development seminars and workshops you will have met them already. They are the delegates who will want to know all about what have you done so far and love to tell you about how much more they've already done.

Or is it you? Are you the one who has to know which seminar they have done and when and what they are going to do next? You need to know that you have done more than they have, because that means you are further down the road to being perfect than they are and that makes you feel better about yourself.

Are you guilty of "keeping up with the Jones's?" You discover a seminar that someone has done that you haven't yet; they seemed to get so much from it that you know you have to do that one, too, in your striving for perfection. Perhaps that will be the one that gives you the tools that will make you perfect?

Is it you that has every book on your shelf? Every CD set, every audio set, every DVD?

Self development is not a fashion accessory! You don't have to wear it and show it off, that's just the marketing departments playing on your need to have it all, be it all, tempting you with wrist bands, pens, and planners, jewelry, books, CDs and DVD sets and, of course – the next seminar!

The Seminar Junkies

Did you accidentally, in your quest for perfection, become a seminar junkie? You fooled yourself in to thinking that in order to be perfect you need to do all of the seminars with all of the big names in the world of self development.

And then you fell further in to the perfection trap because you didn't manage to get perfection from the first seminar, but that's OK they have a Mastery Program; if you do that, perhaps then, you will be perfect. And of course, you hear about the elite group that pays more to spend more time with the guy on stage and you know that you have to be part of that, too. Those are the people who are really on their way to perfection.

Before you know it, you are clocking up the notches on the self development bed post – there can't be many left to do. You have spent a fortune and could well be in a lot of debt as a result. You learned a lot but you didn't apply it all because there was the next one to do first, before you take action. You didn't get the results you want because you moved to the next thing too soon, impatient to get there faster. In the process, you not only didn't get the growth you wanted but now you are really feeling the pressure. The pressure of not being good enough, the pressure of, "They've done more than me," the pressure financially, too.

Aaaaghhh!!! STOP!

That cannot feel good. Self development began by you wanting to become a better person not a perfect person. It's good to stop and remind yourself that.

Take a step back, breathe, and complete this exercise.

1. List the seminars that you have already attended.

2. Thinking about the last seminar that you went to what did you learn?

3. Of all that you learned what actions have you taken to improve something in your life as a result?

4. Of all that you learned what actions can you now take to improve something in your life as a result?

5. If you were to take action on what you have already learned from the seminars, books and tapes would you need to do the next seminar, buy the next book? Or could you be better by taking action from what you already know?

Obsession with perfection can actually cause you to get worse not better.
If you turn self development in to a competition it is easy to become obsessed with what everyone else is doing and the associated "Bling" they have to go with it. You get so distracted by keeping up with the Jones's that you take your eyes off yourself. Instead of the next book being there to read and use, it becomes a trophy. The next seminar is about impressing others rather than improving yourself. Your perfection moves from self development to being the perfect image of self development (in your ego of course) and becomes self defeating because the more you do the less you do! i.e.

The more seminars you take the less action you take, the more books you buy the less you read and do.

It becomes a numbers game, rather than a personal gain.

My advice – if you want to be the best you You can be, turn your attention back to you. Use the resources that you have built up to become even better without having to spend even more. Give up perfection and choose ongoing, consistent improvement. It's so much easier on the sanity and the pocket!

Don't wait to be perfect to share what you know!
The perfection deception also rears its ugly head when you decide that what you have learned is Amazing – "I must share it with others" kicks in and you decide, "I could be a coach, a trainer or run seminars and workshops. I could make such a bigger difference in this world."

Fantastic!! The ripple effect is about to begin…and then perfection makes an appearance and you doubt your ability. Ever had that happen? Brian did.

Brian is a GP who is a little disillusioned with the National Health Service way of running a doctor's practice. He felt that it was too much about targets and budgets and hitting the figures when it should be about patients and their well being.

Brian has done lots of personal and professional development to try to make a difference for his clients but despite doing courses in nutrition and pain management and psychology and counseling, (in fact he teaches counseling skills to others) he still didn't feel that he was making a difference.

Then he heard about Neuro Linguistic Programming and decided that this was something that he could use to communicate much more effectively with his patients, so he did a practitioner level course in NLP. He loved it and got so much more value from it than he ever imagined and really enjoyed the coaching aspects of the course.

I got invited to speak at a NLP practice group about how to use NLP in real life i.e. other than to become a coach and use it. That's where I met Brian and he told me about his dream to open a holistic medical practice one day that would combine traditional medicine and complimentary therapies including coaching and NLP.

As a fellow health professional, coach and NLPer I loved this concept and we got talking. Brian contacted me about a week later to become a client in order to make his dreams come true.

During the first session it became apparent that Brian had caught the perfection bug. He had such plans, so many wonderful ideas, he had really thought it through but he lacked one thing – Perfection. He couldn't put his ideas into action yet, because he was not perfect. He couldn't go and teach others until he was the expert, otherwise in his mind they would not believe what he was saying.

Now think about it - he is a GP, a medical doctor. He has qualifications in all sorts of areas including nutrition, pain management, psychology, NLP, he not only is a counselor – he teaches counseling - and he doesn't believe he is an expert. I have to ask, is he trying to be an expert or is he trying to be perfect? So I ask him this question. "When will you be an expert and be able to start making a difference in the way you have just described?"

His reply, "When I've done a Master Practitioner Course, then I'll feel better able to deliver training and provide coaching." So I check in with that and ask, "So, when you are a Master Practitioner will that be enough, will you be ready to begin. Will you be the expert?" He says, "Well, if I'm going to be training then I will need to do the NLP Trainer course first." "Will you be good enough then?" He replies "Maybe."

Maybe???? Whilst he is trying to be perfect his patients are continuing to suffer and never get the information from him that could really make a difference in their lives! He was waiting to be perfect before he could begin. Waiting for someone to come along and hand him the award that proved he was perfect and could now begin!

You know what?

Permission to be human!

In my world it's better to share something than never share anything!
I'd rather make some difference than no difference. You choose. You don't have to be perfect to share what you know and to really make a difference. We are all works in progress, all on our journeys. You don't have to wait till you arrive there to share the experiences along the way!

What are you preventing yourself from doing because you are waiting until you are perfect?

> "A man would do nothing if
> he waited until he could do it
> so well than no one could find fault."
> *John Henry*

Life is about little truths that reveal themselves along the way.
Here's the thing, whilst you are striving for perfection and experiencing the pressure of that, life is evolving around you little by little, step by step; the perfection that you thought you were aiming for might not be what you want or need in your future reality.

It's that whole thing about everything happens for a reason and you often don't know what the reason is at the time of the event. So an event happens, you declare to the Universe, "That's never going to happen to me again because I'm going to make sure everything is perfect next time!" and off you go on your quest for perfection and protection, not least emotionally.

Meanwhile life goes on and as it does, it begins to reveal little truths along the way – if you are open to receiving them, or should I say, they're there whatever if you are open to noticing them. Or are you so focused on the perfection, so tunnel visioned, that you fail to see the clues, those little gifts that life is giving you that are meant to give you direction, purpose, meaning and reassurance along your journey in life?

Are you aiming for the perfect life? What if it isn't what you wanted when you think you're getting close to it? How will that feel? Keep those dreams and those goals of what you want alive – most definitely I'm a dreamer, give yourself the gift of being flexible to change, new inspiration, new opportunity and new vision.

"Perhaps your mission to be perfect is causing you to play small and what life wants is to reveal the gifts along the way for you to expand who you are even more, not into perfection but into fulfillment."

Actually it's OK to aim for a little perfection when...
I can hear you thinking, "What? After all that now she's going to tell me it's OK to go for perfect!! How can that be???"

Well, my aim is not to make Perfect a dirty word. It's not taboo, (well not quite anyway), I just think that it should be used more sparingly in order to support you, not bash you. So maybe we need to expand our vocabulary a little, to use other words where we would normally say perfect or perfection out of habit rather than intention.

I got my thesaurus out so that I can give you some new word choices to pop into your "Perfect Alternatives" pocket. How about these?

Excellent	Just right	Complete	Fantastic
Precise	Great	Brilliant	Fabulous
Apt	On target	Finished	Incredible
Spot on	Wonderful	Whole	Amazing
Ideal	Just the thing	Accurate	Magnificent

There's a few for starters, take them and practice them, have fun substituting them where you can, see how flexible your vocabulary can become and remember – no aiming for perfection here!

So back to the point at the start of this section – when *is* it **OK** to be perfect?

It's OK to be perfect when you are aiming to be Word Perfect in a play or reciting a poem or singing a song. It's absolutely fine to aim for Note Perfect when you're playing an instrument. Perfect spelling when writing an article, report or even a book is not just acceptable but recommended!

Create a list of things below that that you can give yourself permission to be perfect with, let's keep your craving for perfection happy in an appropriate way!

Things that I can be perfect at:

1.

2.

3.

4.

5.

6.

"Better a diamond with a flaw
than a pebble without"
Confucius

Chapter 4
<u>Live Up To Your Own Expectations</u>

Take yourself back to a time when you were about five years old and remember what it was like when someone asked you, "What do you want to be when you grow up?" Remember that? And you knew you could choose anything at all. Maybe you wanted to be a doctor or a nurse, a policeman/woman or a fire fighter, an astronaut or a teacher, a writer or a circus performer – who knows! You could be anything.

Likewise, when asked, "What do you want for Christmas?" it was so exciting because then you got to dream about having everything too! You would write to Santa with a whole long list of things that you'd seen on TV, or looked at in a magazine or catalogue or you'd seen other people had got. You could have it all – a castle, a car, a flashy bicycle, a helicopter, a princess mansion and beauty parlor, a horse, a truck...whatever your imagination would create.

In those days whoever had asked you those questions would allow you to dream those things and most likely praise you for your vision, but then soon after they start to impart or impose their expectations on you, too. The funny thing is, you accept their expectations of you, especially at a young age, without question. Why wouldn't you? After all, they are the grownups who are supposed to know what's best.

And so it begins, the process of accepting and living up to expectations that were never your own, that you may never have really wanted, didn't know you could object to and that you never actually chose for yourself. In fact, you heard about what was expected of you so often that you began to believe that that was what you needed to do or become in this life as if you did choose it!

Standards

Hey! Nothing wrong with introducing and expecting some standards – people will always rise to the level of expectation you set for them, so set high standards where it's appropriate in order to get the best out of them. Set high standards for yourself, too, to make sure that you get the best of you showing up, remembering at the same time that it's aspirational not mandatory for every minute of every day!

Standards are those rules, if you like, that you set for yourself and others and that others sometimes set for you. The dictionary describes a standard as

1. An accepted or approved example of something against which others are judged or measured

2. (Often plural) a principle of propriety, honesty, and integrity

3. A level of excellence or quality

Your standards are a set of principles that you live by or are expected to live up to and are very often tied into the values that you (or the person setting them) holds most dear. Common values might include:

Love	Freedom
Trust	Health
Honesty	Passion
Integrity	Learning and growth
Being organized	Contribution
Success	Certainty
Wealth	Creativity
Adventure	

Perhaps now is a great time to have a look at your standards and explore where you got them from and whether you want to keep them, change them or remove them from your life. We have standards set in so many areas of our lives from childhood to now. Let's explore some of them together.

1. *Achievements and qualifications*
As you think about your childhood and, in particular, those years at school, that's the time when so many expectations from others are created. Parents encouraging you, or not as the case maybe or perhaps pushing you really hard to get good grades, to excel in every subject or to win at every sport. Teachers, did they bring out the best in you or the worst?
Class mates and friends influence you massively and can bring you with them to success or lead you astray and distract you from studies. I wonder which it was for you?

For me, I loved school and whilst my parents were encouraging, especially around getting good qualifications, they were never pushy or piled on the pressure. I chose my friends wisely and they were pretty studious (without being geeks!) and despite a little appearance rebellion in my teens as I became a punk, it was never a behavior rebellion and I stayed on track. Phew!

Lauren was an ambitious and clever teenager and she knew that her parents had her future sorted for her. "I'll go to university then become a lawyer or a politician," she always told her friends. To her, like her parents, having money and status seemed like everything.

Two years in to a philosophy degree she suddenly started to have doubts. The course work left her feeling stressed and she was surprisingly home sick. She even went to see a counselor as she was suffering from depression.

Her friends and family knew her as a fun-loving party girl and this made it really hard for Lauren to tell any of them about how she was feeling because that was not their expectations of her. As time went on and she really found herself struggling she finally confessed to her mum that she wanted to quit university and come home.

To her parents' disappointment and her friends' amazement she got an admin job and loved it, never regretting the decision to leave university for a minute. She realized that it didn't matter what everyone else thought, it was her life and she was taking control.

2. _Career_

Talk about other people's expectations of you and how they influence your decisions. You know when you get to that point at school and people start wanting to know – what are you going to do when you leave? Well, that was easy for me because I knew exactly what I wanted to do, had known for a long time and that was to combine my love of school with my love of sport and become a sports teacher. Obviously!

But, my dad was not so keen on that idea for some reason and so off I tootled back to the careers office to have a look at what else life might have to offer on the career front and there I discovered pharmacy. I knew nothing about it but it looked quite interesting and the seed was sown.

A few weeks later there was a job advertised in the local paper for a student pharmacy technician and my mum said, "Why don't you apply for it? You might find out a bit more about pharmacy if you get an interview." Seemed a reasonable suggestion to me so I did.

I was fortunate enough to get an interview and me and my friend hopped on the train to Birmingham, a little adventure in itself, as I had never been to Birmingham before. We had a lovely day shopping and I went to my interview. I didn't really find out anymore about pharmacy.

I was lucky enough to get a second interview though, this time at the local hospital so I went with high expectations of finding out more about pharmacy. They didn't tell me a whole lot more either. They did offer me the job.

At that point of decision, I realize now, that I did not have high enough expectations of myself, in that I decided not to stay on at school and do A-levels. I didn't have the confidence in my ability to have done the combination proposed and so I decided to take the job at the local hospital. And so my career in pharmacy began as a student pharmacy technician, never dreaming back then that I would ever go on to do my degree and become a pharmacist.

My friend, Lynn, had parents with very different expectations of her, though. She joined the school just as we started to choose which O-Level qualifications we would do (I know! O-levels – that makes me sound old, they're long gone!) She had been studying in a private school but not getting the grades her parents wanted. Our school had a really great reputation back then, so she came to our school instead.

Lynn was reasonably bright academically; she wasn't top of the class and she really had to study hard to get the grades. In fact, not only did she study hard at school, her parents paid for her to have extra lessons at home, too.

Lynn was not allowed out in the evenings, that was study time. When she wasn't studying English or math she would be having singing lessons and elocution lessons to make sure that she got the best start in her career.

Sometimes we would sneak her out of the house through the bedroom window just to come and hang out for a while, to have a break! Mum and Dad chose her career. Lynn was going to be a lawyer and they were going to push her all the way!

Lynn did stay on and do her A-levels and went on to university to study Law. Yes, she got to Bar School and did become a lawyer and I believe has done very well for herself, I just wonder what she would have chosen if she could have chosen her career for herself.

On the other hand another friend of mine, he went to his careers advisor at the crucial stage in his school life and was subjected to the expectations of a not–so-positive careers officer. In the eyes of the careers officer at this school, boys were doctors, engineers or builders and girls were nurses, hairdressers and mums.

He got to be an engineer, that was the direction he was pointed in and he never questioned it because you just didn't; you trusted the adults to know what they were talking about and your friends were doing similar stuff, so, of course, it was right!

He got the label engineer in manufacturing and that's where the next 30 years of his working life was spent. And then, the bottom fell out of manufacturing in the UK and things got tougher and jobs got fewer and he realized that if he had known he could have chosen anything he wanted back then…or along the way…he would have chosen a different path, who knows! He still might!

It just goes to show how other people's expectations of you influence your decisions at an unconscious level that can affect many years of your life. The good news – YOU get to choose and you get to choose at any time throughout your working life, too. I'm a great example of that, I began as a technician then changed to pharmacist and later became a trainer and a coach.

3. _Roles_

Whose expectations are you living up to with regards to the roles you have in your life? By roles I mean son/daughter, mother/father, aunt/uncle, brother/sister, student, employee, employer, boss, husband/wife, boyfriend/girlfriend, etc. All of those hats that you get to wear through life in your relationships with others.

If your mother was a stay at home mum, who gave up work to look after the kids whilst dad went out to work, the chances are that you as a female took on that expectation: that you should be a stay at home mum, too. Or if you are a man, you may have that expectation of your partner.

Or, maybe mum and dad played those roles because it was expected of them and actually they resented it and encouraged you to be different, to be equal, to go out to work and have a career and share the house work, child care etc.

Maybe you had no strong role models in your family and you took your expectations from other families or from what you saw in films and on TV. Perhaps your teachers expressed their expectations of you in the classroom, about how to be a good student and how to go on to be a good employee. Perhaps, on the other hand, all they could do was tell you how badly you were behaving or performing and they lowered their expectations of you, so you lowered yours accordingly.

At work, did your boss expect you to be punctual, hard working, target driven, precise, proactive? Or did they just let you get on with it, your way, and there were no guidelines so you just did what everyone else did, be that good or bad?

As I'm writing this it's really making me think hard about how much we are influenced by those around us and their expectations of us. How much of it you actually never stop to question and how much of who you have become was not consciously chosen by you. No wonder you feel confused about how you got here and ask, "Is this really what I want?"

4. _Home_

How you are at home will reflect the expectations of others, too. If you were expected to keep your room tidy and help out with the chores around the house then you probably expect this of yourself now and of your kids, too. Nothing wrong with that, in fact I whole heartedly applaud expectations of contribution and taking responsibility at an early age, as long as it is done in a loving way. Doing it in a controlling way will give a whole different meaning and expectation.

If you were expected to let your parents know where you were, who you were with and what time you would be back, chances are you still let someone else know these facts and expect them to tell you, too. In fact you probably get quite upset if they don't.

There would have been expectations around how you dressed and how much TV it was OK to watch, when home work was done and how. You may have been encouraged to have lots of hobbies, you may not. You might have been expected to have lots of friends or not. It might have been drummed into you to always tell the truth and to put others first OR look after Number One because no one else will.

However it was for you at home, then or now, living up to the expectations of others can be a strain if it's not what you have consciously chosen or consciously rejected.

Expectations based on beliefs that hold you back

Quality Standards – Now, if you are in pretty much any kind of business, that's a term you're probably very familiar with. Here, though, I'm talking about qualities in terms of personality traits and emotions rather than a set of specific, concise statements that act as markers of achievement in business.

Thinking about what we have already started to explore in terms of other people's expectations and enforcing of standards, I wonder how many of our personal qualities we absorbed along the way, rather than consciously chose for ourselves too.

A belief is simply something that you heard or said to yourself so many times that we believe it to be true. Whether it is actually true is a different story! At five years old, you may well have believed in Santa Claus and the Tooth Fairy with all your heart and then later found out that they didn't actually exist (sorry if I just burst your bubble there)!

Could it also be possible that there are things that you believe about yourself that might also not really be true? You just heard them so many times that you created a reality around them, gathered evidence to support the belief and now it's who you think you are!

That's the type of belief that will hold you back from discovering your true potential. These are the types of belief that cause you to hold back when you really want to go for it. It's the beliefs that cause you to doubt your ability or your self worth. They are the beliefs that cause you to procrastinate, self sabotage, put yourself down. They limit your growth, they limit your ability and they limit power to be the most amazing human being you can be! No wonder we call them limiting beliefs!

Or, maybe you have some things you do not yet believe about yourself that *are most definitely true*, you just haven't acknowledged them before now and gathered the corresponding evidence to support those new beliefs, too? You know things I'm talking about, the positive things that other people tell you about yourself, like you are beautiful, or talented, or sexy or athletic or brilliant in some way. Those people can see those things in you, just like you see gifts in other people that they don't always believe, too.

Tim always wanted to be a musician. From an early age he was the kid that would drive you mad, constantly tapping out a beat, playing the symbols with the saucepan lids, bashing the toy drums, playing the air guitar, singing into the hairbrush!

He loved music. He especially loved the beat of the music, the rhythm and percussion instruments in particular. As a small child making his music, it was not always appreciated by the adults around him, who would quickly get irritated by the constant banging on make-do instruments around the house.

He would be just in full flow, lost in the beat of a tune on TV or the radio or even just in his head when an adult voice would ring out, "Stop that noise!!!" or, "What a god damn awful racket! Pack it in now!" or, "It's not even in time with the beat – sorry but you've got no rhythm!"

And pretty soon he began to believe it. After all, he was just a white boy and it was the African and Caribbean races that had the gift of rhythm, playing the tribal drums, the steel drums, creating the beat, dancing to the beat. White boys supposedly couldn't dance, so why would they have any rhythm?

He still loved to play but he would practice when no one was around and as much as he practiced over and over, his belief that he was off beat held him back from being any good at it and certainly from playing within earshot of another human being!

Until one day when he was just caught in the moment, playing away to himself to his heart's content and giving it his all just for his own enjoyment, a friend came by and heard him playing along to a band on CD. As the friend walked in to the room where Tim was playing to himself, Tim looked up, embarrassed in the moment, preparing to apologize and before he could get the "Sorry" out his friend took him by surprise.

"Man! That was Awesome!! I didn't know you played the drums! You are amazing! How did you keep that to yourself?"

Tim was stunned, speechless for a few moments as the words sunk into to his thoughts. At first he wondered if the friend was being sarcastic but he could tell by the look on the friend's face that he meant it and there was genuine surprise there. His friend insisted that he play some more and for the first time in his life Tim played to an appreciative audience.

That audience of one changed Tim's belief about his ability in just a few moments. As a result he plucked up the courage to audition for a local band and now plays regularly, loves every minute and gets loud ovations for his musical ability. Oh, and better still, gets paid for doing what he loves!

Let's explore together what you actually believe about who you are and what qualities you have. Here are a few simple questions for you to complete either here in the book or on paper.

1. What qualities about yourself are you really proud of? List them below, for example are you really determined, playful, loving, caring, sexy (!), hard working etc.

2. What qualities about yourself are you not so proud of? For example stubborn, lazy, unfocused, easily distracted, a perfectionist (!) etc.

3. Take a look at the ones you identified for both questions and for each one ask "Did I choose this one for myself or did someone else keep telling me that I was this thing and now I believe it?"

Chose for myself:	Someone else gave me:

4. Have another good look at each and decide, if you could choose right now those positive qualities that serve you, that you know are you or would love to be more of you, which ones would you keep? Write them below.

5. To really ensure that you capture the best of you in a pro-active way write down below any additional qualities, characteristics and emotions that you have inside that you forgot to add to the original list, the ones inside that perhaps you have been forgetting to remember for a while and add those below.

6. It is said when you look at someone else you are looking in a mirror and they reflect the qualities that you also have inside, so what are the qualities that you admire in others that you would also like to reflect to the world?

Set Your Own Standards!

WOW! You have a pretty astounding list of qualities, characteristics and standards right now so it's great to gather all of those things into one statement. Now is the time to set your own standards so that you can be sure that you are living up to your own expectations from now on.

Now is your opportunity to combine all of the things that you have consciously chosen (Woohoo!!) and create your Standards Statement!

Let me give you a couple of examples to guide you but remember you are you; you get to choose your own standards and so your statement may well be very different to these!

TeeJay's Standards Statement

I am a strong, intelligent, independent, passionate, woman who is enthusiastic and energetic each and every moment of every day.

I am love – I LOVE life and love being me. In my feminine energy I am loving, caring, compassionate, giving, confident, sexy, positive, playful and powerful.

I am a passionate lover.

I am a loving wife.

I am a wonderful mother and caring daughter.

I am a loyal friend.

I am a driven career woman, entrepreneur and business leader.

I am an awesome, inspirational coach.

I am a leader, a mentor, a role model, a teacher.

I am a perpetual student in this game of life.

I am courageous and focused – a goal setter and getter.

I go to give and not to get in all that I do.

I am full of joy and SO blessed in my life and I am grateful for every gift that is bestowed upon me.

I am beautiful, soft, and open. My energy, vitality and gorgeousness radiate from me and draw people to me.

Emma's Standards Statement

I am "The Force" - I determine my own fate with the help of my understanding, with God, and with my Higher Power

I am the Bill Gates of my own Life - 'how do I create the intelligence that runs the entire Labyrinth?'

I am passion, excitement, enthusiasm, curiosity, to take on what I need to take on.

I am a geek

I am an astrologer

I am a social BLAST when I want to be. I am fun, sarcastic, and humorous.

I am inspiring and confident (<<== At last I feel a strong glimpse of that last one!)

I am a student and a teacher

I am intelligent and analytical

I am a caring individual committed to take action to protect and serve, myself first to make sure that I am taken care of, then extending that out to others.

I am a mother...

I am nurturing and caring and their rock of emotional security and I am always willing to guide those to better decisions in their lives. I nurture with love, care with firm guidance in accordance with my own growth, and I provide the most optimum emotional security by letting them know that they always have my ear and my guidance.

The guidance I provide is in direct proportion to the personal growth I accomplish. After that, it is their responsibility to follow through with their own decisions and actions.

I am an Achiever - I decide, I plan, I commit, I take action, and I get results.

I am a music lover - I enhance my relationship with myself through the music I cherish.

I am a daughter

I am a sister

I am a good best friend

I am becoming a person of Integrity more and more every day, who walks her talk (almost) daily, and a person worth modeling.

I am The High Priestess

John's Standards Statement

I am wealthy- surrounded by it every day

I am prosperous- for myself and others

I am an awesome -health/wealth/prosperity magnet

I generate great things for myself and others

I exude Joy/Love/ vibrant energy

I am fit- lean, serene, purple, karate machine

I have laser focus- engaged in my interests, not in distractions

I have a wildly successful biz

I work with groups on bettering my corner of the world

I have sharpened my abilities to avoid "pot holes"

I repel negative energy- spirit suckers beware!

I dance, sing, and kick butt with Grace & Style

I gather with amazing people

I am a skilled architect of life

I solve problems in places of great need

I share my healing with those who are still suffering

I have huge reserves on many levels

I am wise & persuasive

I am a black belt

Susie's Statement

I Susie am amazing and blessed beyond my wildest dreams. Abundance and wealth surrounds me always. I am a bubble, a bubble of love, of light and of laugher. I share out all my gifts to others near and far. I am laughter, the five year old Susie who giggles and plays through the day.I am loving, I am caring and I am loyal - a fantastic daughter, sister, friend and girlfriend. I shine, sparkle and shimmer, an inspired me. I am focused, a leader and an entrepreneur in all I do. I think outside the box, I am innovator I am successful. I am a budding, growing trainer and coach, excited and a dreamer. I dream big and achieve big. I live with passion, purpose and drive and ambition in every moment of everyday. Every time I breathe I rejoice that I am alive, that I am fit, that I am healthy, vibrant and energetic. I am adventurous, I am fearless and free. I am spiritual and free, connected to my source always. I am comfort and relaxed, I am a child of god and I am in spirit. I am a centered, strong and confident feminine energy. I am sexy and beautiful, fashionable and amazing and I am lust! I am love. I am light. I am laughter.

Now it's your turn to have fun creating your own Standards Statement. One that is unique to you because you are unique. Take all of the things you wrote down in the exercise above for questions 4, 5 & 6 and combine them together as creatively as you choose to design your own Standards Statement.

Remember to state it in the positive and use "I am" because "I am" is a very powerful statement to the unconscious mind. "I am" proclaims your identity and the unconscious mind has no choice but to be congruent with the identity that you give it. "I am" gives it the direction to follow – the standard to achieve.

If you say, "I am excited!" the unconscious mind say, "Woohoo! I'm excited let me be that now." If you say, "I am depressed," the unconscious mind says, "Ok, I'll be that now." If you say, "I am successful!" the unconscious mind says "Excellent! I'll be successful now" You get the idea right? Great – so create your own statement choosing your "I am's" carefully.

My Standards Statement

Step into and Expand your Greatness

What I love about setting your own standards and expectations of yourself is that you can review them, adapt them and raise those standards any time you choose to, in order to keep yourself growing and moving forward in an enjoyable, inspiring way, without the pressure of trying to be all things to all people and attempting to be perfect in it all, too.

Keep your Standards Statement with you all of the time, put it on your phone and a note in your wallet or purse so that you can remind yourself often of who you are. Let it really integrate and become you and then perhaps in 6-12 months come back and revisit it to expand it or raise those standards as you wish.

"Our deepest fear is not that we are inadequate. Our deepest fear is that we are powerful beyond measure. It is our light, not our darkness that most frightens us. We ask ourselves, Who am I to be brilliant, gorgeous, talented, fabulous? Actually, who are you not to be?

You are a child of God. Your playing small does not serve the world. There is nothing enlightened about shrinking so that other people won't feel insecure around you. We are all meant to shine, as children do. We were born to make manifest the glory of God that is within us.

It's not just in some of us; it's in everyone. And as we let our own light shine, we unconsciously give other people permission to do the same. As we are liberated from our own fear, our presence automatically liberates others."

Marianne Williamson

I believe that each and every one of us has a Greatness within us; the first massive leap forward is to accept and believe that of yourself and to step into your greatness. You do this by doing the exercise above – weeding out the things that do not serve you and embracing the things that do, writing your standards and then living them.

Once you have stepped into your Greatness and you are enjoying the process of growth and change that that brings then you get to expand your Greatness by allowing yourself to explore new possibilities about how amazing you are and how powerful you become when you find your truth. I dare you to have fun exploring how incredible you really are!

"The vision that you glorify in your mind, the ideal that you enthrone in your heart. This you will build your life by, and this you will become"

James Lane Allen

Chapter 5
<u>So What Do You Really Want?</u>

Now that you have started the fantastic process of becoming the person you choose to be, it's time to really support those choices by setting some goals. Now I know I run the risk here of you slipping back into perfectionist mode but by now I'm trusting that you have well and truly got the message that it's not a good idea and that it's possible to achieve, without the pressure of perfection. So let's go for it!

I love to set goals, have that thing to look forward to and to keep me inspired, challenged and growing. I love it even more now that I get to set my own goals rather than having goals imposed up on me. Now that you have set your own expectations and standards you get to choose your own dreams too – how brilliant is that?

The Power of Focus
The clearer you are about what you want, the more likely you are not only to achieve it but also to achieve it quickly. The unconscious mind, that part of you that runs your body without you even having to think about it, loves to have something to focus on. It allows it to get to work your behalf, to filter out all of the things you don't need, to complete the outcome and highlight all of the opportunities and resources that you do need, to get you there faster.

It's a bit like this….
If I was to tell you that you have a target and give you a vague direction for it, then blindfold you and spin you around, then give you a bow and arrow and ask you to hit your target…oh and throw a few arrows at you while you try it, because after all, that's what life does isn't it? How likely are you to hit the target?

Very unlikely.

If though, I were to give you a big, clear target right in front of you with no obstacles in the way, no blindfold on, no spinning around - well, that would be a whole different outcome, wouldn't it?

What you focus on is what you get – so focus on what you do want, not what you don't and allow your unconscious mind to support your journey.

What did you do with your Dreams?

Now is the time that you get to dream your own dreams again and do it without the perfection pressure, too. That is such an exciting gift to give yourself and I realize, too, that for many people it's actually not that easy.

When I first started to get into goal setting I thought Great! This is easy! All I have to do is set some targets, write them down, read them daily, take some action and I'm there! Magic!

And I did just that. However, in order to continue the momentum of achievement, once you have realized that first set of goals and you're now moving on to the second or third set of goals I realized that they were all short term, they were all do-able and they were all a bit ordinary.

Someone said to me that I should set longer term goals and that I should dream bigger. And at my first attempt I realized that not only did I find it hard to envision further than one year ahead but I had the blankest mind ever when it came to dreaming big!

I realized that I had forgotten how to dream past the ordinary. I had forgotten what it was like to let go and let my imagination run riot, like I did as a kid, when everything was possible and there were no limits.

Where did that ability to dream go? As I thought about it, I realized that, once again, other people had enforced their beliefs up on me and caused me to lower my expectations, to the level of their expectation. I had had dreaming conditioned out of me and replaced with, "Get real!"

It breaks my heart when I hear the dreams of children being squashed. Not so long ago I was out shopping. It was summer time and so the supermarket was full of outdoor things for holidays and lazy afternoons in the garden. I heard a little girl in the store asking for this toy, that book, a trampoline, a fish pond, a swimming pool, a chess set, garden games, tennis racquets, barbeques, a tent and… And then I heard her dad say – "For goodness sakes! You can't have everything you know! Just stop asking."

Aha! How many times as a child do we have our desires squashed, our imagination mocked and our dreams kicked into touch? No wonder as we grow up we learn not to dream anymore! I realized there and then that in order to get past my goal setting block I needed to learn to dream like a child again. To go back to the age that I put my dreams on the shelf, where the "Get Real" adults had forced me to put them. I needed to take them down off the shelf, open them up and play again!

At what age did you get fed up of being told that you can't have everything you want? Did you finally listen, too, and give up your dreams? It happens to most of us at around seven or eight but the secret to having an amazing life is to dream BIG! So let's go back to where we left them and learn to dream all over again.

It was a little strange at first but once I found the memories of how I dreamed as a child, it got easier and easier. Pretty soon my dreams were unbelievable, totally unrealistic and very EXCITING!! Yay! Those are the kind of goals to have!! That's when the real magic begins to happen and you realize that you can live life on your terms and have whatever you want in it!

So where did you leave your dreams? Go back into the child inside you and find the excitement that you had as a child, before Christmas or your birthday, dreaming of all the amazing things you had on your list of presents. Nurture your imagination, remove all boundaries, take off the shackles of realism and just let your imagination run riot! The sky's the limit? Why? Who said there had to be a limit? That's the way to set goals!

The Invisible Link

"When you are inspired to dream and that dream becomes a physical entity by writing it on paper something magical happens. An invisible link is formed between thought and reality and without needing to know the 'How' your dream can come true!

I met a fellow business adventurer this morning at a networking meeting and we got talking about goals. He said, "I'd never really set goals throughout my life, until about nine months ago. At that time I really wanted something more from life and my business and decided to get serious about it. I set two goals, with deadlines and really focused on them. Within nine months I had achieved them both and they weren't lightweight goals either! I thought WOW! This thing really works! I'm not sure how – but it works!

That's what I love about goals. If you set them with a belief that you can achieve them and a commitment to making them happen you don't have to know the HOW! In fact – as a friend of mine would say, *"The How is none of your damn business."*

There's something quite magical that happens when you capture a dream, write it down and commit to it in your heart. It's like an invisible link that is formed between your thoughts and desires and the material world. Expressing that thought and making it a physical thing by writing it onto paper that you can touch, feel, see and carry around with you makes it already real even before you see it unfold.

Dream that dream vividly, every day, and the universe will conspire to make it so. You will have just the right flashes of inspiration, meet just the right people at the right time, find opportunities all around you that you never noticed before. With a passion for your dream will come new depths of emotions that will propel you toward your goals – courage, confidence, joy, energy, determination, assertiveness, intelligence and discipline - each one there to guide you and fuel you to this new destiny.

At a goal setting session recently a gentleman wrote down that in the future he would not only like to continue to exhibit his paintings, but to sell them, too. He kept those goals to himself but wrote them down and took them with him.

The next time we met he was so excited to tell me that he had really enjoyed the goal setting session; it had really made him think and he had got a lot out of it. He confided that one of the goals that he had not told me about was the one about the paintings. He had had three paintings in an exhibition locally; he had left them there whilst he was on holiday.

When he got home he popped over to the gallery to pick them up and to his amazement there were only two left! They had sold one for him whilst he was away; his goal had already being achieved in his absence! Fantastic.

If you're not convinced yet, here are another couple of examples of how when you set goals magic just happens...

When my youngest daughter was about six years old, like every six year old little girl or boy she would watch TV and enjoy the adverts as much as the programs. At that time there were a lot of advertisements for Disneyland, you know the ones with the princess's castle and the parade and the fireworks, the Magic of Disney.

She passionately wanted to go to Disneyland. Every time it would come on the TV she would ask, "Mummy, please can we go there?" and of course I would say, "Yes, one day we will." Who am I to squash her dreams with my reality? My reality, at that time being a single parent with two children, a big mortgage, and so many commitments that I had no idea when that day would be. I did however, write it down in my long term goals and then kind of forgot about it.

Later that year my dad is round at my house. We're chatting and he says that he's at a bit of a loss as to what to do. It's my mum's 70th birthday in a few months time and he doesn't know what to do for the best. Does he organize a party for her? He really feels he needs to make sure that such a special birthday is acknowledged and celebrated.

He'd like to organize a surprise party but would she like a surprise party? If he organized a party and let her know would she be disappointed that it wasn't a surprise party? Would she really want a party or something else?

Gosh, what to do for the best. So I say why don't you just ask her what she'd like to do? That way, well, it might not be a surprise but at least she'll get what she wants and you can't get it wrong.

My mum decided that she would like to spend her birthday with her family. We are quite a small family, my mum and dad, my older brother, his wife and two children, myself and my two girls and my younger brother. We're kind of scattered around the country a little and so don't get time to all be together very often.

She decided that she'd like to spend time with us, not just to get together for a meal, but for a holiday. A long weekend somewhere just the ten of us somewhere that she had never been before. Yes, you guessed it, my mum decided that she would like to spend her birthday with us all at Disney as her guests; she paid for us all to be there.

So my daughter got her dream, my mum got her birthday wish and my goal got ticked off the list much sooner than I could ever have imagined. Sometimes goals are achieved without you having to do anything to make them happen other than think them and write them down. You don't have to do the How.

Here's another example….

Just the other day it happened again. I discovered some music by a composer called Ludovico Einaudi. His music is beautiful, enchanting, music that inspires, takes you away on a magical journey, soothes your soul. Just wonderful. I love it and have been not only playing it all the time, but raving about it to everyone I meet!

So I'm raving about it to a client and I get all excited and say, "Actually, you know what, I'm going to put it on my list of goals, I would love to go to a concert by him. Wow! That would be amazing, imagine, listening to him play live. That would be awesome!"

The very next day I get a text from my client asking for ideas on how to celebrate a goal that she has just achieved. I was in a meeting and couldn't reply straight away so I read it intending to reply as soon as I could. Before I could return that message I get another one from her saying

"Gosh, the universe works quickly on helping with that "How to celebrate" thing. Guess who's touring the UK in November? Care to join me to see a certain Mr. Einaudi in concert? My treat!"

I am stunned! Really? No way. That's incredible. The very next day! Which just goes to prove two things:

1. Dreams DO come true and
2. The How is none of your damn business!

So whether you believe it or not this stuff works. Why not try it for yourself?

It's all about balance
If you are to have any chance of staying human instead of going off, once more, into a perfection mode, then you have to make sure that you retain some life balance. I am talking about balancing goals in different areas of your life of course, AND more than that: I am also talking about balancing the go-getter goals with the give-me-a-break goals; the serious goals with the life's-too-short-to take-it-all-seriously goals; to mix being centered and focused with being able to let go and laugh at yourself.

To do that, you have to set goals in a range of areas and aspects of your life. That could be career, business, finance, relationships, hobbies, leisure time, self development, health and so on. Balance is about harmony and synergy between the different areas of our life and the roles that we get to play.

If your goals are balanced you get to be healthy enough to wake up early with the energy you need to propel you through the day. If you keep fit, then you get rid of the possible stress that built up whilst you were focused at work. If you have career goals, they keep you moving towards your financial goals. Your financial goals allow you to enjoy the rewards in life.

You can't enjoy the rewards in life if you don't know what they would be for you. You also can't enjoy the rewards if you have no one to share them with, so having relationship goals are just as important as rewards. And of course you can't enjoy any of that if you are not fit and healthy enough to take part in these activities.

Balance. It's not about running between the poles to keep the plates all spinning, it's about creating a harmonious set of outcomes that each supports the other to expand who we are, what we do and who we get to share it all with!

Start thinking now about some of those areas of your life that maybe you need to be spending more time in and less time in, and those areas where you can relax and enjoy just being you.

Let's set some Goals!
The best way to do this is to grab some paper and a couple of different colored pens, if you have some handy. Find yourself some music that you love to listen to, that makes you feel great and inspires you. Then give yourself the gift of about an hour to two, to enjoy this process of creating the future to your expectations and standards.

Are you ready? Excellent! Let's begin by just taking a minute to remember what it was like to be five years old. Five years old, it's the night before Christmas and you are so excited. You have written to Santa, sent that list of everything that you want and you know that everything and anything is possible. Feel that sense of anticipation and expectation as you remember what you saw that night, what you were saying to yourself and how it felt to be that child who dreamt of having it all.

There are no limits to your dreaming and you don't need to think about how any of these things will happen. "The How is none of your damn business," just write it down. I know sometimes when you set goals it's easy for the reality speech to butt in and interject your dreams. It's like having two little voices, or two little characters, one that says, "I really want this," and the other that says, "but that's not real." It's like they sit one on each shoulder, isn't it?

Well, here's what to do. When you hear the one that says, "but how?" The one that says, "you can't have that, you can't do that," – you have permission to gag it! When it starts to intervene imagine it's there on your shoulder and just knock it off!

Flick it away – It has no place in this process.

Read through the following steps first of all to get an idea of how we are going to set these goals together. Once you have read through them set yourself some time, I would suggest at least two hours to go through the whole process.

We will set goals in just three specific categories today, because if you have too many categories there is a danger of being overwhelmed.

By the end of the exercise you will have your top three goals for each of the three categories. I believe that nine goals are more than enough to focus on at any one time. All of the other goals will be there to progress to once you achieve those nine in the next twelve months or sooner.

Actually, by keeping the number small, just three categories and three goals from each, you will be amazed at how quickly you will achieve them and be on to the next lot! That's both the power of focus and the magic of dreaming!

Part 1 – Identify Your Goals
Put that music on, grab your paper and for each of the three sections use the length of one track of your music, one song, to write down all of the things you would love to have in that category. Keep your pen writing for the whole of the track. Remember – you get to dream, dream big, no limits, no "Hows" and definitely no perfects!!

Personal Goals
These goals include personal development, books you might like to read or listen to, courses you might like to take for your own enjoyment. Relationships – what new friends would you like to have? Would you like a new or improved intimate relationship? Better or different relationships with family? Physical environment, i.e. where you live, work, and spend your time – how would you like those places to be?

And health - would you like to have lower blood pressure or a healthier body? Would you like to have more physical fitness or endurance?

How will you contribute outside of yourself? Will you give time, money or the skills that you have to make a difference to others who are more needy than you?

Career/Work and Financial Goals

These goals are for you to design your work and wealth goals. Do you love what you do and have goals to expand that in some way? Do you want to do something new and different instead? Do you want to work for someone else or be your own boss? Are you a budding entrepreneur or do you want to be the best employee you can be? What sort of company will you work for or set up? How many people will work with you? Where will it be?

How much do you want to earn.... A week, a month, a year? How much money would you love to have in your bank account? When do you want to retire? What investments do you want to have? Property, gold, stocks and shares? What will it be for you?

"Stuff" Goals

Here you get to choose the stuff that you want in your life, you know, the rewards, the gadgets, the jewelry, the techy stuff. The things that make you smile, allow you to relax, make life easier, more entertaining or just plain self indulgence. The boy's toys and the girl's accessories! You could also include here holidays or places you would love to travel to, concerts, the opera, perhaps you'd like to be pampered on a regular basis with spa breaks, and massages and manicures and facials.

Maybe you'd like to climb a mountain or swim with the dolphins or wing walk or have a balloon ride or just enjoy a quiet picnic or walk somewhere with someone you love. Do you want a different home? A second home? A holiday home? Would you like a swimming pool or a pool table or a trip to Table Mountain? It's your dreams, your choices...no limits, remember!

Part 2 – The When

Now you get to choose when you would like these things in your life by. Go through your lists and in different colored pens write the following by each goal.

Within 1 year write a 1

Within 5 years write a 5

Within 10 years write 10

More than 10 years write 10++

Part 3 – Prioritize the 1 year goals

For each of your lists, go through your one year goals and identify the three most important for you to achieve this year. Write these on a separate sheet of paper. You will end up with nine goals in your list.

Part 4 – The Why

Grab nine sheets of paper or have nine pages ready in your note book. At the top of each page you are going to write the name of each of your nine goals, one per page. Put some more music on and for each goal answer the following questions:

O Imagine this goal already achieved and write down how it makes you feel to have accomplished it. What does it mean to you emotionally? What will you go on to do because you did that? How will it impact you financially to have that goal? How will it affect the people around you? Why do you want it?

O What will it cost you if you don't get that goal? There you are in your rocking chair reflecting back and noting your regrets....you didn't achieve that goal. How does that make you feel? What has it cost you emotionally and financially? How did it affect the people around you? What did you not go on to do as a result of not following through with this goal?

o What resources do you already have to support you in that goal? This might be resources in terms of your strengths e.g. determination, courage, confidence, intelligence etc. It might be resources in the equipment you have, information available or people you know or have access to.

o What resources will you need in addition to the above?

Remember to repeat the above questions for each of your nine goals.

Part 5 - Take action!
Congratulations! You did it!! You dared to dream, have written your goals and have them there before you - a bit like putting each one on a stage in front of you – see them there up on that stage that is your stage, your future. That stage at the moment is movable, portable, mobile – you get to take your goals everywhere with you. Just like any stage it has a set of steps that lead up to it to get you there – except at the moment the 1st step is missing and it's too far to the second one to actually step up to the goal.

If you don't put in the first step – you may end up pushing that stage around with you forever without making the journey to the goal. You need to make sure that you get the first step so you can make your dream come true. So for each goal write down one step, one action you can take within the next 24 hours that will take you that 1st step toward your goal. Get to climb the steps from there to achieve centre stage – the celebration of the successful completion of your dream.

A Question a Day for a Step a Day
Ask yourself each day as you get ready to begin that new day, "What one thing can I do today that will take me one step closer to just one of my goals?"

It doesn't have to be a step a day for every goal - that could also cause you to feel overwhelmed - so just identify one thing every day that you can do that will move you forward. It can be a small step, it can be a big step, what matters is it's a step forwards.

121

Choose who will be your biggest raving fans!
I know that you are so excited to have all of these wonderful things to look forward to and that you'll be bursting to share your goals with others. A little word of advice before you go rushing out to do that! Choose wisely who you will share your dreams with, because there will be those who will not be so enthusiastic to see you change and grow.

Let me tell you about the frogs. Every year somewhere around the world there is an annual frog marathon. You might not know about it, it's not very well publicized yet but it happens every year. The frog marathon isn't your normal run 26 miles around a city, oh no, it's much more than that. The frog marathon takes place in the tallest building in the chosen city and instead of 26 miles, the frogs run up 100 flights of stairs.

This year's marathon actually took place just last week and it was a very special occasion indeed. The frogs all arrived at the venue and gathered excitedly in the reception, limbering up and stretching and psyching themselves up for the race. And along with the frogs and their supporters you always get the hecklers don't you? The hecklers in this event are always the toads that turn up, envious that they don't have their own event and they're not allowed to enter in this one.

> "Don't know why you're bothering
> to even turn up – you'll never
> make it past the start line!"
> *They taunt.*

> "Give up now you'll only embarrass yourselves,"
> *They shout.*

> "You don't have what it takes,"
> *They jibe.*

The starting pistol fires and off they go up the first flights of stairs and the toads hop into the elevator to get there before the frogs, so that when they arrive on the landing of the second floor, the toads continue their torrent of negativity.

"Harder than you thought isn't it? Admit it, you're not up to it!

"You're just like all the rest, all talk, you'll never make it!"

And sure enough some of the frogs gave up and dropped out of the race.

The rest of the frogs continued on and half of the original group got to the 30th floor. Here, sure enough, waiting on the landing outside the elevator were the toads. The toads were really enjoying discouraging the frogs now, especially as more and more of the frogs got disheartened and gave up.

"See," they told them, "We were right, you can't do it. You're not fit enough, you're not determined enough, who do you think you are?"

And more and more frogs gave up, after all, it had never been done before, no-one had ever yet managed to get to the top, so perhaps the toads were right, maybe it is impossible. Perhaps they were wasting their time. Maybe they should just get real. As the race continued, surely enough, the numbers got fewer until finally there was just one frog left.

One lone frog and he just kept going. The toads continued to heckle and taunt but he just kept on. Totally focused on getting to the 100th floor. The toads were amazed, in fact, everyone was amazed and with each flight the excitement began to build. Wow! He might do it! He could be the one to get to the finish.

Finally, exhausted and exhilarated that single frog made it to the top. The crowd that was waiting there for him cheered so loudly you could hear it throughout the building. The reporters lined up to ask him, "How do you do it? What's your secret? Did you train for months?" But they got no answer from the frog. Assuming he was just catching his breath they gave him a minute or two then the questions began again. But no reply. A few of the toads began their heckling again.

"Typical of a frog - too rude to answer. Too full of his own importance to lower himself to speak to the minions."

Then one reporter, who knew the frog, taped him on the shoulder, turned him around, looked him in the eye and signed to him, "They want to know, how did you do it?"

Hmmm. Maybe sometimes it's an advantage to be deaf!
(Or simply not listen).

There will be those who will say, "Yeah right! Who do you think you are? You'll never do that. I know so and so, they tried that and it didn't work." I know you know the people I'm talking about in your life. Those are the people you need to turn a deaf ear to, just like the frog or simply not share your goals with in the first place. Pick just one or two people who will support you, cheer you on, be your biggest raving fans all the way to the goals and celebrate it with you. Those people who will encourage you and kick your ass into touch when you start to doubt, give up or become stuck!

Visualization – Your Amazing Mind

Your mind is an amazing, powerful and creative tool. With it you have an awesome capacity to change how you feel long-term, by creating your future right now.

> "If you can imagine it,
> you can achieve it.
> If you can dream it,
> you can become it."
> - *William A. Ward*

You not only have the ability to remember events and re-run them in your mind, but you are also capable of creating events or feelings in your imagination before they actually occur. You do this all the time, when you are looking forward to a holiday you have booked or when you have planned a night out. You think about how it's going to be and build up an expectation of how it will play out don't you?

Athletes use this ability to practice their techniques and to run the races before they have even stepped out of the starting blocks. Golfers use it to practice their swing, musicians use it to practice their performances before the big day. The incredible thing is -- and I love this – the mind can't tell the difference between what is real and what is imagined vividly.

Wow! How cool is that? If you imagine your future vividly – it becomes your reality.

So if you want to feel fantastic, have tons of energy, be happy, successful and abundant in every good way, the secret is to start that process right now in your imagination. How?

Everyday set aside ten minutes each morning and ten minutes every night to do this. Sit quietly, close your eyes and let the process begin.

In your imagination see yourself as the person you would **LOVE** to become.

Where are you?

Who are you with?

What are you doing?

How does it feel?

Breathe deeply and soak it all in.

Now make the picture brighter, add more color to it. What are you saying to yourself or others around you? Make the feelings stronger, feel the emotions you're feeling more intensely. Smile as you see yourself being amazing, as you feel an incredible inner strength, joy and confidence! Now turn the sound up. Make the vision even more real!

As you experience the joy and passion of who you are, give thanks for it as if it has already happened, as if it is happening right now in this very moment. Celebrate the new you! Celebrate the moment and make it real. Do this over and over again, for all the ways you want to change, for all the new things you want to do, for all the new, powerful feelings you want to experience. Live the life you deserve, the way you want to **NOW** and you will be well on your way to making it your reality!

Become "Bouncy and Bendy!"

I love that thought – it conjures up such fun images! What I mean by it is this. Being bouncy is about having fun along the way. Enjoy the process of getting the goal; be excited and energetic as you get to do something amazing. Bounce out of bed every morning because you have something exciting to focus on and be passionate about and you can't wait to take the next step.

Allow yourself that gift of excitement as you realize that dream. Approaching each part of the journey full of beans, lively and effervescent, realizing that each little step is an achievement by itself, so you get to have mini celebrations along the way. It's not going to be perfect so you can take that pressure off yourself straight away and just enjoy.

Be flexible in your approach, realizing that you don't have to do everything – you can ask other people to help along the way, in fact, asking others to play a part gives them a gift because everyone likes to help someone. It's not always about how you get there but that you actually do get there!

And just because you don't get the result you expect does not mean that you failed, it just means that you got a different result from the one you were expecting. Simply ask the question, "What can I learn from this, how can I use it to my benefit and get on with the next approach."

Bouncy and Bendy!

Have fun and be flexible!

And remember to give yourself
permission to be human, too!

Get Creative!

One of the things I love to do when I set goals is to be able to see them as well as read them, so I create a dream board or what others might call a vision board! It's great fun to do and if, like me, you are very visual, you'll love to look at it every day and be reminded about all of the wonderful things you're going to get to do.

So how do you create a dream board? Easy, you get a big piece of paper, A3 sized is brilliant, and you look for images of what you want in your life either in catalogues or magazines or on the internet, and you put them together like a collage on your paper. You can add drawings or text here and there or quotes maybe to inspire you. It's your dream board, you get to create it the way that you want it and you can add things to it at any time.

I know some people create dream boards that show all of their goals, others have one for relationships, one for health, one for hobbies, one for career etc. That's up to you. I have mine up on the wall in my home office, where I see it every day.

You might choose, instead (or as well as), to create your dream board on your computer and have it as your screen saver or desktop so that every time you turn on your computer, you are reminded of your goals.

What I also love to do is to create an achievement board. That's the one that I put on all of the things I have achieved already, so that I can be reminded of the amazing things I have already done and enjoy the memories of them again. Photographs, copies of published articles, copies of certificates or letters, or my first paycheck for a new contract etc. Magical memories that I can enjoy at any time.

When you have it, remember to Celebrate it!
Woohooo!! You did it! Whatever "it" is for you. And it absolutely does NOT have to be perfect to know that you got there and celebrate its achievement. Make sure you stop and really acknowledge yourself when you reach the goal. Pat yourself on the back, let people know that they can congratulate you too, celebrate it with a treat or a reward of some sort before dismissing the success and rushing straight on.

You could celebrate in any number of ways. Here are a few suggestions and you can add even more of your own.

Go for a meal with your partner, friends or colleagues

Treat yourself to a spa weekend or a massage or a manicure

Buy yourself that gadget, gizmo or jewelry that you've wanted for ages

Do something outrageous like sky dive, wing walk or bungee jump

Go to the theatre, a concert or a movie

Treat yourself to a night in by yourself with a good film, book or friend

Go out dancing

Book a holiday or a day trip

Take the day off and sleep in late, then have a lazy day for a change.

Go paint-balling or quad biking

Go and see your favorite team play and take your friends with you

What will you do to celebrate? Write some ideas down below of things that would be a celebration for you.

"The reason most people never reach their goals is that they don't define them, or ever seriously consider them as believable or achievable. Winners can tell you where they are going, what they plan to do along the way, and who will be sharing the adventure with them."
- Denis Waitley

Chapter 6
Take Your Foot Off the Gas
if You Want to Go Further!

There is a danger when we go into perfectionist mode to become so obsessed with getting it done perfectly that we lose sight of things around us, people around us and sometimes even the goal itself.

The Tunnel Vision Trap

In that quest to be perfect and knowing the power of focus in getting things done, there is a danger of getting stuck in the "Tunnel Vision" trap. You know the one; the one with the excuse that you are laser focused, determined to get there and nothing and no one will prevent that. You won't stop until you have it.

So you go full out, it takes over every thought, every action, every conversation, and every waking and sleeping moment. You've heard that "other people" work all the hours God sends to get the job done – that's dedication and commitment for you - so you think you have to do the same because that's how to be perfect, or to get the business to be perfect, or to get the house to look perfect, or to study hard enough to get the perfect grade.

You keep going, relentlessly, not listening to your body, not listening to those around you, refusing to be distracted. You get so tired but you have to keep going. You know you need to take better care of yourself but that can wait. You should go and get more exercise but you haven't got time right now. Got to stay focused, get it right, do the right thing, keep going, battle on.

The Great Escape

That tunnel vision in one area of your life might be an escape route, a way of not facing one area of life that's not perfect by concentrating all of your efforts on an area that you are good at, that you enjoy more or that you feel more significant in. Let me make my work perfect because my home life sucks!

I went there, did that and got the t-shirt! I had been married for about six years when I realized, one day, that I had fallen out of love with the man I was married to. I met him when I was at college and he was working there. There was chemistry and attraction; he was a gentleman and treated me like a princess. He was the bread winner, I was just a humble student and so he got to take care of me. All was well and we moved in together quite soon after we met.

My friends became his friends and we were together for four years, going on to buy a flat together, then a house and it was kind of just expected that we would get engaged, get married and of course that's what we did. I had finished my course, started work and began to earn about the same as he did. All was well, we were equal now and I could give something back.

After my first year at work I got promoted and enjoyed both more responsibility and more money. We moved house again and money was tight so because I could earn the much needed extra more easily, I volunteered myself for some overtime. Then I began to notice, the more I did the less he was prepared to do and I began to resent it.

The more I did, the more I learned and got promoted again. More responsibility, more of a challenge, better pay. I started to realize that the more I did, the less he did and I resented it even more. I felt as though I had to do it all because he wasn't pulling his weight. He wasn't treating me like a princess anymore but like a slave!

The more I felt dissatisfied with him and my home life, the more I threw myself into my work. At least at work I was respected, important, making a difference. At least at work I was learning and growing and enjoying the company of the people I worked with. At work I felt I could be the real Me, so I spent more and more time there, with the excuse to my husband that I was a perfectionist, so I needed to put in the hours.

In reality it was my great escape. A way of running away from things not being perfect at home. And the more I ran the worse it got at home, of course. In order to cope with things not being perfect at home I rationalized in my mind why I was staying in the relationship. I had some great stories to defend my actions... or inactions as the case may be!

I would tell myself that it wasn't so bad really, he worshipped the ground I walked on, I could be so much more badly off. We had children together, you have to think of the children in this and the effect splitting up would have on them. He didn't beat me, abuse me or control me. To the outside world we had such a good life. He was a good father. I'd said my vows before God and swore I would only marry once.

Oh and more, I could give you so many more excuses for why I was still there. Unhappy at home and living my dreams through my job. Life has a way of catching up with you, though. It drops hints about what is not right, what you should consider and where you should go next. If you take no notice of it, ignore it, and rationalize it, it has a habit of taking matters out of your hands.

Life will sometimes give you a wake-up call to force your hand. If you are not going to take action to resolve things, life will! That's what happened to me. The company that I worked for had discovered and whole heartedly embraced personal development, sending its top managers on a three day course called, "The Seven Habits of Highly Effective People." The brain child of Stephen Covey.

Being the over achiever, I decided to buy the book and read it before going on the course. I loved it! For the first time I realized that personal development could apply to my personal life and not just my career. I totally embraced its concepts, or habits and really looked forward to learning more on the course.

Day one, towards the end of the day, the trainer closed the curtains and got all of the participants to lie down on the floor. He put on some music and guided the senior managers lying there on the floor with me that day to an imaginary meadow. We floated above the meadow with its babbling stream and the blue sky away in to the future.

The trainer's words took us out in to the future to create our futures just how we wanted it to be. Imagining where we were, what we were doing, where we worked and lived and who was with us in that future. See it all clearly, hear what's going on around you, really feel it all. I can hear his voice right now.

After the exercise the managers were all chatting excitedly, discussing what an amazing journey they had had and how brilliant it was. How they saw their husbands or wives sharing their success and how they couldn't wait to call them later to tell them all about it.

I didn't join in with that chatter. I couldn't. I had had a very different experience as I floated out in to the future. Sure enough I could see the future. I knew exactly where I was, what I was doing and who was there with me. It was as clear as day. The only problem was that my husband was not there with me. I felt guilty about this and had tried my best to imagine him in there somewhere, somehow. But it was no good, he just was not there and there was nothing I could do to make him be there.

For me, my life had just been tipped all over the carpet in that hotel conference room and I was left to pick up the pieces. It was time that I faced it – I no longer loved the man I had married and I needed to finally address things.

I left the course vowing that I would take six months to do everything that I could to make things right again. To take responsibility and to try to regain the love and romance but if at the end of the six months I still felt the same way, then I would have to make the decision to leave. I deserved that and so did he.

As the six months went by I got more and more into personal development. The great escape grew in many respects, as it was now not just escaping at work but escaping at home too, escaping in to books and tapes and CDs, anything that would help me to put those pieces of my life back together again.

Sometimes, though, just like Humpy Dumpty, it can't be put back together again and you have to use the pieces in a different way, to sculpt a new life instead.

The end of the six months loomed and I got more and more unhappy, knowing that I had to decide what to do. One Sunday morning I couldn't bear it anymore and took myself off into the countryside to make my decision.

As I walked around the lake that day I realized that I needed to finally be honest with myself and with my husband. You have one life and you need to live it as you, the real, authentic, honest you. Living a lie, escaping to work was not living as my true self. I had to leave the relationship and discover who I really was.

Later that day I took a deep breath and told my husband that I did not love him anymore and that I was ending the marriage. He was shocked. It came out of the blue for him, which surprised me; I thought he would have guessed things were not right because of my recent mood swings and distance. As hard as it was, it was done. I knew beyond a shadow of doubt it was the right thing to do and I have never regretted it for a second.

"The Great Escape was over
and the Grand Adventure
was about to begin"

Significance and Recognition

That tunnel vision, the perfectionist approach can have its rewards of course and that's why you can get sucked into it. When you start to show commitment and raise your standards, people notice. They give you rewards in the shape of recognition, praise, awards, and significance and it feels amazing.

It feels so good that you want more of that external feedback. Who wouldn't? The danger is though that it can be a bit addictive and it's easy to start to rely only on external recognition and validation to know that you are doing a great job, instead of having the confidence and self assurance to know within you that you are doing a great job.

The perfectionist approach fuels the yearning for more people to say great stuff about you and you get caught in that trap. Now you start to feel bad if you are not given credit so you focus even harder on getting it right, getting things perfect, to get the good feeling when people notice you.

The challenge with this is that perfection becomes the fuel you need to get the results and as you get results the pressure mounts up to do even better next time. Good becomes expected, so in order to get the level of recognition you want you have to outperform yourself and do better. Perfect is not good enough and you strive for more; the pressure keeps building until the stress becomes unbearable and something has to give.

Being all things to all people

If you didn't get caught in one of the above Perfection traps, did you get caught in this one? Or, worse, maybe you did get caught in one of the above perfection traps and this one! That is, thinking that in order to be the perfect person you have to become all things to all people.

Yes! We have a large number of human beings attempting to be "Super Perfect Human Beings!" but whose expectations are you trying to live up to? It's that question again, isn't it? Are you living up to your own expectations or those being imposed up on you? I hope that after the exercise on living up to your own expectations, you are now deciding to do just that. If you did not yet do the exercise, I suggest that you go back and do it right now, to make sure you know whose expectations you are attempting to fulfill with this madness of trying to be the perfect person!

Gentlemen, is this you?

Must have a good job

Must be the best at that job by pleasing the boss, the employees and the share holders

Must have the best results in that job

Must be the most liked employee and/or boss

Must maintain my ideal weight by keeping fit and working out daily

Must lift more weights than him

Must run further than him

Must be funny and make people laugh

Must be a leader

Must have a beautiful wife/girlfriend

Must be seen to have the perfect marriage

Must have 2.4 children

Must be the best dad

Must have the right car with the right image

Must have the right hobbies

Must socialize in the right places with the right people

Must be masculine oh and show my feminine side when appropriate

Must be the gentleman and also show equality

Must be fearless with the lads and caring at home.

Ladies, is this you?

Must look my best at all times
Hair - Make up - Nails - Clothes - Shoes - Accessories

Must have the perfect house, even if that means getting up super early to get the house work done

Must have the perfect kids, must make sure they have it all

Must make sure I stay in shape by dieting and exercising

Must be the perfect wife - efficient and organized and taking care of everyone's needs

Must be sexy

Must make sure I have a job and do my part to bring some income in

Must have the best job

Must be the best at my job

Must get that promotion

Must be liked by the people I work with

Must be in control

Must be sociable and have lots of friends

Must invite those friends over to be sociable, too

Must be a great cook

Oh, and they say I should have some hobbies too. Must be the best at those hobbies.

Who needs a man? I can do that!
It's my job to take care of everybody

I'm exhausted just writing it, let alone doing it all!

In business, especially if it's your own business you feel the need (who's need I wonder?) to check the boxes:

Work long hours

Be available at all times

Have the "Blackberry" permanently on

Get a dongle so that you can be online on your laptop from anywhere, anytime

Network with other businesses as much as you can
Breakfast meetings - Lunch meetings - Evening meetings - Online forums - Twitter - Facebook - YouTube - Myspace

Hold teleseminars

Webinars

Write a book!

Then you have got to have products
Articles - Ebooks - CD's - DVD's

Run courses

Be the Expert

Find your niche!

Remember to do the marketing too
On-line - Ad words - Newsletters - Email campaigns - Direct mail - Lumpy mail - Traditional adverts - Flyers - Brochures - Trade shows - Speaking engagements

"Show me the guy who wrote the rules for perfectionism and I'll guarantee he's a nail biter with a face full of tics... Whose wife dreads to see him come home!"

Charles Swindoll

You know what? I love to be the best I can be. I love to do the best I can do AND I love to recognize that I am not a perfect super human being. Allow yourself permission to be human. Whilst you are concentrating on being all of these things to all of these people, what is happening on the inside to you?

I hallucinate that the answer to that will be that you are beginning to feel stressed. You feel resentment that you have no time for you. You are exhausted, frustrated and gritting your teeth, just to get through the next part of the day. You don't sleep well because there is just so much to do, think about and get perfect. You are a walking time bomb.

Time ticks as the pressure builds one wrong look, word or gesture you're likely to explode on a scale that is inappropriate to the circumstance and it could all come crashing down around you, leaving you and the people around you to pick up the pieces and begin again from scratch.

Gotta be the Best

Actually not just the best but the Best! Nothing else matters, no one else and nothing else counts when you get in to this trap. The competitive streak goes into over drive and there is no cruise control and no off button. It becomes obsessive and drives your every waking thought and probably your sleeping ones too!

You have got to be the best no matter what. Rational thought can go in the drive to be the best. Whatever it takes, no-one can get in the way, no-one can stop you, you are getting to the top, the best, perfection like it or not, taking no prisoners, get on board or get out! You make a lot of enemies along the way but who cares? They don't understand. You are a perfectionist.

140

Friends try to tell you to slow down
– *they don't understand.*

Relatives start to raise concerns about your health
– *they're just overreacting.*

Colleagues start to avoid you
– *that's their problem not yours.*

You're not sleeping well
– *you've just got a lot on your mind.*

So much to do to be the best
– *that's just the price you need to pay.*

Battling on Causes Fatigue

I know that that might seem like stating the obvious. It's amazing how you can get caught in the above traps and not realize that you are so focused on the perfect that everything around you is further and further from that perfection that is so important to you. So I feel the need to remind you that battling on causes fatigue!

Not convinced? Let's examine it further.

A friend of mine, Ian, joined the company as a Regional Retail Manager. It was a position that was much sought after and he was very pleased to have been awarded the role, in the face of steep competition. Of course, he wanted to make a good impression and he was both ambitious and conscientious. Eager to please his new boss, impress his colleagues and make a name for himself within the company.

The role he took on was a new position that had been created as part of a restructure within the company, as it got ready to expand. Ian had the chance to shape the role, lead the way, set an amazing example. He wanted his results to be the best, for his stores to be outstanding, for his reports to be perfect.

Every store visit he did was meticulously researched in advance. When he arrived, he took the time to speak with every member of staff to get their views and to build rapport. He consulted with every member of the regional team before, during and after the visit. He would spend hours perfecting the visit report that he would submit to the company following the visit.

For every Regional Retail Manager meeting, every Regional team meeting, every Head Office meeting that he was required to present to, he would have the perfect PowerPoint presentation, with every detail included as appropriate. He would provide reports and handouts and give detailed recommendations about how that project should be progressed.

Ian was always the first to arrive and the last to leave. He would volunteer for any project that would put him in the spot light and give him the opportunity to be recognized. He was always pleasant, friendly and well mannered to ensure that he was well thought of and liked by everyone.

Perfect!

Or was it?

You see, in order to do all that, be tunnel-visioned, be all things to all people, to be the best and be so focused required both a lot of time and energy.

Something's got to give....

Ian worked long hours, not just at work but at home, too. It was not unusual to receive an email from Ian at midnight, or 2am or even 4am. Not just now and again but on a regular basis. It took time to do all that research, collate that information and write those reports. It took time to get the perfect pictures to put in to your PowerPoint presentation and to make the handouts interesting.

He still had calls to make at work that meant he had to check and reply to emails in the evenings. He made sure that everyone had his email address to encourage them to contact him at any time, with any questions, so people did. This meant that he had lots of emails to read and reply to at the end of the day - and being the perfectionist, he had to reply to them all that day.

No matter how long it took, he would work until it was done. It was his reputation at stake, so now it had to be even more perfect. Working late soon became the norm, a habit. He expected it of himself and others were now expecting it of him, too.

Relationships....

When you are so focused and working so hard for such long hours, that has to impact on your relationships. It certainly did for Ian. Ian had a wife and three young children, the youngest just a baby. He wanted to spend time with his children but would often get home from work after they had already gone to bed. They hardly ever saw him, except maybe on weekends.

At weekends he would make some time to spend with the kids but only a little while and all the time he was with them he would be thinking about the work he should be doing, how behind he was getting. He was with them physically but they knew he wasn't there emotionally and they felt that, too.

His compromise to spend time with his wife was to work on his laptop in the evenings in the lounge. Again, there in body, definitely not there in any other way that she needed him to be there for her. She felt neglected, unloved, rejected, even, and resented it.

His friends had stopped bothering to call because all they got was a list of reasons why he couldn't possibly go for a drink, play a game of squash, meet up for a chat. Similarly couples he and his wife used to socialize with felt that they were not welcome any more and they got fed up of the fact that all he would talk about was work. It was all he knew!

Working long hours takes its toll on your ability to be patient, rational and reasonable and so inevitably the likeable, patient, friendly Ian began to get tetchy, impatient and didn't suffer fools quite so cheerfully any more. His colleagues began to notice this and tread a little more carefully around him as the months went by.

He hated this because he was no longer as perfect as he had intended to be and he beat himself up about it, vowing to work even harder to put it right. His relationship with himself and his own self worth began to be affected and he put himself down on a regular basis, telling himself how useless and lazy he was. Not good enough, must try harder.

Health....

When you're putting in those many hours and pushing yourself that hard, the first thing to go is often the most important time – that is time for you. You haven't got time to go to the gym, it takes too long. By the time you've got there, got changed, done your exercise routine, showered, got changed again and got home, well, goodness!! That's way too much time used that could have been spent doing that additional research, answering those emails, writing those reports!

No time for that!

And as for healthy eating, well, that just takes too long, too. When you've got things to do, no time for breakfast, gotta get out and get on with it. Lunch for Ian was a sandwich on the go, as he traveled between stores or it got skipped if there was no time even for that. The only healthy meal he got was his evening meal cooked by his long suffering wife. Not that that was at its best by the time he got home and it had been ready for hours.

He began to swap his bottles of water for energy drinks and his cups of tea for strong black coffee to keep going. Not realizing that he was becoming more and more dehydrated and poisoned by the caffeine he was ingesting. He started to get palpitations and sweats, not to mention the indigestion and acid reflux he was experiencing, too.

He looked pale, his complexion suffered and he looked like he was going through the whole teenage spots crisis, all over again. He looked clammy as the caffeine caused him to feel queasy and perspire. He was exhausted, had black rings under his eyes; the expression, "He looked like death warmed up," springs to mind.

Focus....

The very thing that he thought he had most of began to slip as the exhaustion, dehydration, poor nutrition and stress fogged his brain and he found he couldn't concentrate in the same way he used to. He would make mistakes and get cross with himself, that he had to go back and correct it. Not only did he find himself doing work over and over but it took twice as long, too. So now he was working twice as hard to get less done at a lower quality.

Relaxation...

Relax? No time for that! The only relaxation he got was when he would fall into bed, exhausted, for just a few hours sleep, so that he could get up early, to catch up what he didn't get done late the night before.

Do you recognize yourself in Ian's story?

I can't help but wonder if you have ever found yourself in the same trap as Ian, whether this could easily have been your story, too? I know that it's something that I can be so guilty of. Getting so caught up in what I love to do and achieve, in my desire to grow my business and in my passion to serve other people, that I can drive myself too hard and become completely out of balance and exhausted.

It's OK, now and again, to get an important piece of work done but it is not sustainable longer term without a severe impact on your health, your relationships and your quality of work.

I need to finish the story for you, too.

It was a Thursday and Ian had been involved in meetings all week, driven to a lot of different locations and covered a lot of miles. He had had little sleep and was by now completely exhausted; not even the energy drinks and caffeine could stem the fatigue. Today he was at another store meeting 200 miles from home; he left home early and was driving home late.

His colleagues were concerned that he looked so tired and suggested he stayed over in a local hotel that night but he insisted that he was fine and needed to go home to get stuff done. As he set off on his drive home it was late, it was dark, it was raining and he was fatigued. He didn't notice the lights coming towards him as he fell asleep at the wheel and collided head on with a lorry.

Ian woke up in hospital many weeks later, very lucky to be alive, very damaged by the accident. The doctors were concerned about brain damage and thought that the injuries to his spine may mean he would never walk again. Suddenly work didn't seem so important after all. He was lucky to be alive.

How is battling on affecting you right now (or has in the past)?

Take a few minutes to give that question some thought. Jot your answers down below and ask yourself was it worth it?

It's OK to pause – Pausing is not giving up!

Attempting perfection is detrimental to your health and mental well-being. You can get so caught up that it becomes an obsession, addictive; the routine becomes a habit, the norm. Putting in all that focus and effort actually makes you less efficient and takes you further from that perfection, not closer. So why do you keep going?

Fear of taking a break

The concept might seem a bit odd but no one said there was anything rational about this. I know people who won't stop because they're afraid that if they do they might not get going again. They'll lose momentum or interest or procrastinate, so they have to keep going.

For others taking a break means that they are not determined enough or good enough or resilient enough, so they view taking a break as being a failure. The ego will not allow that and so they carry on to prove a point to themselves and others.

For other people, they are just afraid to let go, even just for a little while, in case someone sees it as a weakness or an opportunity to step in, take over and get the credit for their hard work.

Take a minute and think about yourself. What fears come in to your mind when you think about stopping what you are so engrossed in? Write your thoughts below.

Effects and Effectiveness

Ian's story clearly shows the impact that battling on in that quest for perfection can have physically, mentally, socially and intimately. As you sacrifice yourself for the impossible, you also sacrifice those that you care about along the way. And for what? To be even less effective than you were before the obsession began!

There comes a time to press life's pause button, to stop and think objectively and to re-evaluate. I would like you to have the opportunity to do this before your story becomes a drama like Ian's story, or like Jenny's.

Jenny is the manager of a small business in a large group of businesses. She has been there for many years and watched as the business went from being owned by a private individual that she knew personally and worked with, to being taken over a number of times until it had been swallowed up by a very large national chain.

As she had been with the business from the early days, she felt a tremendous loyalty to her team and to her customers and she was also feeling the enormous pressure from the new management to do even better. Being a bit of a perfectionist, she wanted to ensure that everything was always just so in the store, as it reflected on her as a manager and her reputation was important to her.

Her team had not been getting on well over that last year or so and a lot of negativity had crept in. Morale was not good and a particular member of staff had had a lot of time off sick, so the others had had to do extra to cover for her – reluctantly. Jenny was finding it harder and harder to motivate them to do what was expected, let alone go the extra mile to meet her exacting standards.

Now Jenny was doing the extra work to cover for her team, going in early to tidy things up, put things right, print off and complete paperwork, so that head office didn't see that standards had dropped. She was working late, catching up with the jobs that had been left or sorting out errors and complaints. She was sick of the constant negativity, all the moaning and groaning and blaming of other people.

Jenny was worn out and worn down! Finally when she hit rock bottom she came to see me. She had tried to be perfect, run the perfect store, have the perfect team and not achieved any of those things. She was disillusioned, exhausted and had had enough; she was ready to quit. She came to explore other avenues, other careers, set other goals to attempt to escape her current job and feel better about herself again.

We explored other options, other careers and we did set some goals but the most significant and effective thing that Jenny did was to take a step back, pause for a short time and take an objective look at the situation at work. Actually, in reality she took a step up – onto a chair! I got her to stand on the chair and look down on the situation as if she, her store and the team were all there in miniature below her and she could see the whole picture.

As she looked down on the scenes playing out below she began to realize, finally, how it had all started to get out of control, why it was being perpetuated and, most importantly, to come up with options and strategies to put in to place, to put things back on track.

Jenny soon began to realize that the problem was her perfectionism and that sometimes her demands on the team had been unreasonable, that her approach in dealing with staff members, when they didn't quite hit her standard, was critical and unappreciative, so the staff began to resent it and morale spiraled down.

She got that the more she did for them, the less they felt valued and the less they wanted to do. She also got that the more hours and the more of their work she did, the more resentful she got of them and yet it was of her doing.

She understood that in order to achieve the standards she aspired to; she needed to change her approach and lead her team, train them, delegate to them and appreciate the value they added. She needed to make the changes within herself and her approach, first.

Within a matter of a few weeks Jenny had turned around the situations at work and realized that she didn't want another job, or another career: she had just needed to get her life back! Now she was back in control and trusting her team, rewarding them for the work they did, gently guiding them in the right direction when they needed it and leading the way with positivity and encouragement, not to mention more smiles.

She decided where she was, was where she was meant to be and now she could enjoy it again. The bonus was that they were getting the results that she had wanted all along, too, and she got more time, now, outside of work, to pursue the new goals she had set for herself.

So climb onto a chair and look down
Perhaps it's time to take a step back and see things from a more objective point of view. Imagine stepping on to a chair for a moment and seeing yourself standing in front of you doing the busy, busy, focused, battling on thing. Imagine that you can shrink that "you" down to a quarter of the size and see yourself down below there, much smaller now and see everything that is going on around you, that you couldn't see before because it was just too close.

Look down onto the scene and take in just what is happening to you and all around you, as if you were a fly on the wall, or as if you were a reporter from a newspaper, asked to go and get an overview so that you can write an article about it.

As you take in all that is occurring, notice how is it affecting you and the people around you?

If that was someone else and other people below you, what advice would you be giving?

Capture your thoughts and advice in the space below or on some paper, if you prefer.

Time to recharge those batteries

If you really want to work effectively, efficiently and maximize the amount you do in the time you have, you simply have to pause to recharge the batteries on a regular basis.

When you think about it, it makes perfect sense but caught up in the madness, there is no sense. It's only when you can take that step back to be objective that it becomes clear. People, as well as things, work so much better when they are looked after, given the right fuel and better taken care of, with ongoing maintenance!

It's like using a razor to shave yourself. If you keep using the same razor, over time it gets dulled. The more blunt it becomes the more pressure you have to apply to get it to shave the hair and the more likely you are to get cut or get razor burn. You need a sharp, undamaged blade to cut cleanly and safely; it's not good to keep using the one that's got blunt or been dropped on the floor and broken.

If you want to get your goals, you have got to look after yourself. If you want the energy to work a little harder some days, sleep a little less on occasion and play full out when you need to get something done, then you have to be proactive about your health. That means taking time for yourself to eat a healthy diet, drink at least two liters of water a day and get some exercise.

Take the time to go to the gym, go out for a walk to get some fresh air, or to go and be pampered once in a while. Have your hair cut, get a manicure and/or a pedicure, sit in the sauna and relax. Go for a swim or walk the dog, simply sit and meditate for 20 minutes or even take a power nap!

Which reminds me, please make sure you give your body the gift of sleep every night. I do not believe that we all need 8 hours; on the contrary I believe it's different for each person and on the whole we need less than that if we are eating properly, hydrating and exercising.

There is a theory that you sleep in 90 minute cycles and that at the end of the 90 minutes is when you naturally wake. Therefore aim to sleep for multiples of 90 minutes, i.e. an hour and a half, 3 hours, 4 ½ hours, 6 hours or 7 ½ hours. Doing it that way you'll be waking naturally and feeling so much more refreshed than being rudely awoken by your alarm, just as you go into a deep sleep and then you wake feeling groggy and tired.

It's amazing that, when you take the time to look after yourself, re-energize and change your focus from what you were so engrossed in, when you do go back to that project or job or whatever it was for you, you enjoy it so much more. You get so much more done and you can be so much more creative in it.

Make a list below of the things that you will now do to make sure that you take the time each day to look after yourself and to re-charge your batteries.

Back to balance

As well as re-charging those batteries and changing your focus for a while, each day it's important to get the balance back in your life. You saw from Ian's story just how many things got abandoned in his life so that he could have more time for his work. When you concentrate so much on one thing and ignore everything else, life has a habit of tipping you over!

Quite literally, in this story that I heard recently about Lady GaGa. Apparently she was so sleep deprived, which she attributed to jet lag, that she passed out on stage three times during one performance. She said, "I'd rather die on stage than walk off the stage because I was going to pass out. It's never happened to me before, I was just really tired."

That is your body trying to communicate with you, to let you know that you not only need to recharge but you need some balance back, too. Is any career, project or goal so important that you are willing to sacrifice not only your health and your relationships, but your life, too?

You need to plan time into your week to spend with family and friends. Fun time, time to socialize, intimate time with your partner. Time for hobbies and learning and creating. Time in the garden, maybe, or time out in nature, where you can breathe again and appreciate the wonderful gifts around you. Time to go to new places or enjoy new experiences. Take a picnic to a local beauty spot or go to the theatre or the opera. Enjoy listening to, or even, perhaps, playing music or singing or dancing.

There are so many incredible things to do and to enjoy to bring balance back into your life. List the areas in your life that you need to do more of to regain that equilibrium, bring back some stability and make life so much more interesting and enjoyable again.

How to pause for a while

We have talked about the fact that it's ok to pause for a while and the benefits of doing that but how do you pause for a while when you are so used to battling on?

Stop the "To Do" lists and start a "Get to Do" list!

In my experience "To Do" lists have a certain pressure associated with them. It's like a never ending list of things that continues to grow rather than ever be finished. As satisfying as it is to tick things off that list, you never get the fulfillment of getting to the end!

It's like a silent master – haha! Literally a Task Master! And it never says thank you, it just keeps asking for more and more of your time! I personally am not a fan of something that mentally beats me up when I read it. It perpetuates the perfectionist model, as if your life cannot be perfect until the list is complete.

I have opted, instead, for a kinder, more balanced, more user friendly, more human type of a list. I call mine the "Get to do" list. It's a list of all of the possibilities that I have to choose from, when I choose to change my focus and keep myself balanced and energized. I look at it and it creates, for me, a sense of anticipation and excitement as I look to see what I get to do for a while, instead of what I was doing.

On my "get to do" list I have all sorts of things that I would love to do. Some things are steps towards my (balanced) goals. Some things are just relaxing things, such as to go and meditate or listen to a favorite piece of music. Some things are little jobs around the house that won't take very long to do and will distract me and change my thoughts for a little while. Some things might involve looking after my health, some things might nurture relationships, like to call a friend or arrange to meet for lunch, or send an email or a text.

I have big things and little things. Important things and fun things. Things that take a day, things that take an hour, things that take 5 minutes. Some things get ticked off because they are just one-offs, other things stay on because I like to do them regularly. The things in my "Get to do" lists add variety to my day and value to my life. It gives me choice, so that even when I do need to knuckle down and get something done, that requires me to be on task, I can still give myself permission to be human, too.

Create for yourself a "Get to do" list, either below or on paper, or maybe on your phone or pc. Include things that you love to do, are fun to do, get things done around the office or at home, allow you to relax, nurture relationships, allow you to learn and grow and include some of those things that have to be done, too.

The Perfect Day!

I feel the need to add, here, that if you are tempted to turn this into a perfection project **STOP!!** This is not an exercise to create your perfect day; this is an opportunity to delight in all of the wonderful things that you get to experience as a human being. It's about expanding your experience not perfecting it.

If you are scheduling every activity in at a particular time of the day – **STOP!!**

This is a "get to do" because you *can* rather than you must. It's a way to take the pressure off yourself, not a way to add more pressure. This is to make sure that, instead of striving for perfection that leaves you unfulfilled, you get the chance to do things that allow you to feel human again and will give you satisfaction and a sense of fulfillment.

"Just as your car runs more smoothly and requires less energy to go faster and farther when the wheels are in perfect alignment, you perform better when your thoughts, feelings, emotions, goals, and values are in balance."

Brian Tracey

Chapter 7
Modeling
(Without the Airbrushing!)

If you are serious about becoming the best you can be in any chosen skill, career, or maybe a quality you wish to nurture, then you need to know about modeling. Both from the point of view of being able to accelerate your growth in your chosen area and in passing on those skills to others, too. Find roles models, become a role model and learn the art of modeling, to combine lots of different best bits into who you are, to become the best human being you can be.

What a role model is....
A role model is someone that you look up to, admire and want to be like, in some way. Good role models inspire you to become more that you thought you could be and bring out the qualities within you that you might not have known you had. It's someone who has an influence on your behavior and beliefs in some way.

Of course, there are positive role models and negative role models around us all the time. I'm trusting that you will be picking the good examples to model and the bad examples to learn from about what not to do! Role models shape who we become as individuals right from early childhood; you didn't know it but you were modeling even back then. Now it's time to do it actively, rather than passively.

One of the people who I deliberately chose to most influence me when I was younger, was a lady that I worked with at the hospital. I was just 16 when I started work there, intelligent, eager to learn and also very independent and a bit of a rebel. I think that Agnes recognized the good in me and the potential for going off the rails, too, and she took me under her wing in a very gentle and humble way.

Agnes and Tina were the pharmacy department bottle washers! In those days everything was dispensed into glass bottles and when they came back from the wards they were washed, dried and recycled by these two ladies. They were both in their late 50's and were salt of the earth women. Honest, hard working, genuine and caring. They worked mornings and were always there before any of us, they cheerfully just got on with what they did and if you were passing or working in the vicinity they had a wonderful way of inadvertently dispensing a little of their wisdom to you, in the conversation.

At the age of eighteen I was pregnant and happy to be so. I thought I was all grown up and ready for it; I had left home, I lived with the father, it was a deliberate choice. Unfortunately my parents were not so keen on my choice of partner and the day that I went to their house to tell them the news of my pregnancy we had a huge argument, I stormed out of the house and walked the four miles home and they were none the wiser to my condition.

That was January 1st and my baby was due in July. I got back to work after the New Year break and happened to be working in the pharmacy unit where the bottle washers were stationed. The two ladies were shocked to hear about the argument and very concerned that my parents did not know that I was expecting a child. They tried to persuade me to call and tell them but I was eighteen and stubborn and there was no way I was going to do that. So instead, Agnes in particular took me under her wing and became my "Mum No:2"

Over the next twelve months I was privileged to get to know this remarkable lady who was so humble and yet possessed such greatness. This lady had the most amazing heart and capacity to love, unconditionally. I discovered that she had been pregnant a number of times but either miscarried or the babies had been stillborn. As a result of her experiences, she quietly raised money for the special care baby unit at the hospital we worked at and would give that money, anonymously, much of the time.

159

She and her husband did finally have a child; a little boy whom they adored. Tragically, he developed childhood cancer, a form of cancer that was aggressive and, certainly in those days, not curable. He had lots of treatment and they did their best for him but sadly he was taken from them at just four years old.

Instead of feeling bitter about it Agnes and George decided that they had so much love to give to a child that they would foster instead of trying for another child of their own. They fostered many, many children and a large number of those children have stayed in touch with them over the years, sending pictures of their children sharing their blessings. Some still send Agnes cards on Mother's Day to say thank you.

Agnes loved fostering and had some challenging children through their house at times but she loved them all. Still longing for a child of their own, they decided to adopt. I remember Agnes telling me about the day they went to the hospital or adoption agency to decide which child they would choose.

She said, "I looked around and there were so many beautiful children in that room, each one very special. And then I saw a little boy, a baby boy who was of mixed race and I knew that he would be the one who would be left there the longest as he was not as pretty as the others and his skin color would go against him. I chose him because he needed us most."

They loved him so much and whilst they didn't have a lot financially, they gave him all that he needed emotionally. Time flew by and the boy grew in to a man. A man who, unfortunately, got in with a bad crowd and caused Agnes and George a lot of heartache but they always stood by him and met his needs. He got married and he and his bride lived with them until they could afford a place of their own. And then they moved out but things didn't work out and they got divorced, dashing Agnes's hopes of becoming a grandmother.

160

A few years passed by and Agnes's mother came to live with them. She was quite elderly but very sharp minded and Agnes doted on her. Her mother would go the local "Darby and Joan" club, a club for senior citizens to enjoy socializing, recreational events and leisure facilities. In fact, I believe she met a gentleman there when she was in her late sixties and re-married.

Unfortunately, he was older still and became ill, passing away a few years later, leaving her widowed again. As well as raising money for the special care baby unit, Agnes also made things that she would sell to raise money for the Darby and Joan club, too.

In the mean time her son met a girl and they moved in together; the relationship grew and they had a child together. Agnes was elated, finally the grandchild she had longed to have in her life, to love. She adored him and spent as much time with him as she was able to.

Now, life is interesting isn't it? George, the love of Agnes's life and childhood sweetheart, has the most beautiful soul but was perhaps not the most handsome of men. His top lip was disfigured and also had a deep red wine stain birth mark covering it. Agnes, of course, only ever saw the beauty within this man and he was wonderfully caring and kind hearted. What is interesting, though, is that the grandchild, who remember was actually not a blood relative, bore a similar red wine stain birthmark over his lip.

As soon as the little boy was old enough, Agnes paid for him to have laser treatment to remove the mark, so that he would not have to grow up with people staring at him or judging him for it. Shortly after that fate took a twist and the couple split up. It was not amicable, it was not pleasant and Agnes and the little boy got caught in the crossfire. Agnes was denied access to the grandson she loved and adored so much and had waited for so long. She was brokenhearted but never bitter or resentful towards the ex-girlfriend, always just hoping that one day things would be different and that she would see the little boy again.

Returning to my tale of how I got to learn so much about this amazing lady, it was because she loved so many people so much. She could not stand the thought that I would go through my pregnancy, such a special time, without my mum there for me. She hated the fact that I would not tell my mum that I was pregnant and yet she never made me wrong for it.

She would check in with me every day to see how I was doing. She was there for me when I was excited about having my first scan and feeling the baby kicking inside. She was there for me when my hormones kicked off and I would be over-emotional for a moment! And she was the one who persevered and finally got me to see reason and to at least tell my mum she was going to be a grandmother.

I finally did call my mum just a few weeks before I was due to give birth. Yes, she was shocked. Yes, she stood by me. And yes, she loved my daughter unconditionally. So it was a very short pregnancy for my mum and dad, as it had been Agnes who had shared the ups and downs of it all with me and we had grown really close.

When my daughter was born, Agnes came to see me in hospital, something that she never did normally when friends or relatives had babies, because it was painful to remember her own babies that had never come home. She loved my daughter and became not only Mum No 2 to me but like an additional grandmother to my daughter, too. I have so many wonderful memories of sunny afternoons with Agnes and George at their house with my daughter and their little dogs, that they loved so much.

Agnes was such a great influence in my life. She showed me what being humble was. I learned how amazing it was to give generously in a quiet, unassuming way that was never about ego, always about love. I got the gift from her example of how to see people for the wonderful souls that they are, not to judge them by their looks or their actions. She is a role model that I will forever be grateful to have had in my life and 26 years later, we still stay in touch.

What a role model is not....

A role model is not perfect! Role models are human, too, and whilst they may be fantastic in some ways, they will have their "humanness" in others, too. The fantastic thing is that when you have a role model, you get to choose the aspect that you want to do better and model that – you don't have to become a carbon copy of them: modeling is not cloning.

Being a role model does not mean becoming a perfect person, either. Often we may become role models for others without knowing it; not everyone comes and asks for permission to model you. In fact, most people don't do they? But they can be very influenced by your actions and beliefs so it's worth thinking about who you want to be in what company, especially around children.

Who are you a role model for and why?

Write down below what qualities or skills do you have that other people would benefit from modeling?

Who are your role models, either now or in the past and why?

Mix and match models

Because there is no such thing as the perfect person, there is no one person that you can model. You get to pick and mix. You get to have different role models for different skills, qualities and behaviors that you would like to have more of within you. The great thing about modeling different things from different people is that it makes sure that you keep you in the mix, too. You add to who you are, instead of attempting to become someone you are not.

It's a bit like going window shopping, you see something you like and you put it on your list.

Glenn is a young man that I have the pleasure of knowing through the work that I do as coach, trainer and chair of trustees for www.innerflame.org, a charity that inspires young people to discover their true potential. Glenn is a co-founder of the organization and was just eighteen years old when I met him. In the time that I have worked with him, I have been consistently impressed by his enthusiasm for learning and his ability to put his learning into action.

He is one of the few people I know who have embraced the concept of modeling so fully and accelerated his learning as a result. As we are talking about modeling, here, it dawned on me that there was no better person to share his story than Glenn. I asked him to share with you his experience of modeling others: what he wanted to model, why he wanted it and the role models that he chose. I asked him to share with you what went well, what he learnt and what he's now doing differently as a result of his learning.

He wrote this piece for me so conscientiously and brilliantly that I have chosen to keep a part of it in Glenn's words, here in my book. I want you to hear it directly from Glenn and model him if you wish! So here it is...

Glenn's Story, Glenn's way

I look to my desktop clock and it reads 00:05 am. This isn't an unusual time for me to be up and focused, then again it isn't unusual for anyone my age to be up at this time on a Friday night. Perhaps, then, the difference is how I am spending my time, while my peers are out on a night out, content to kill as many brain cells as humanly possible in one night; I am satisfied to be sat at my laptop, about to share with you what being around some of the greatest minds in my life and, more importantly, the greatest people, has done for me, with the intention that you will see a value and take those first steps to doing it for yourself.

This hasn't been an ordinary night. Up until 10:30 pm I was reading, reviewing and evaluating a document that could potentially change my life forever. An ambitious and innovative US based software start up are requesting that I join them, in return for equity in the company and a potentially handsome salary, as a member of their management team.

My focus is spent switching between thinking how cool is this? A bunch of Fortune 500 execs want me to join their venture and the fact that my close friend and mentor, who in his 60's, is using Google Docs to collaborate on the document, whilst Instant Messaging me with invaluable feedback. This man is a great friend that I would never have met if I had not taken the step and simply asked to model him. One of my greatest life decisions.

The picture would have looked very different 18 or even 24 months ago. I was confused and had no belief in achieving what I wanted. I denied what I wanted to other people and sadly even myself. I had no conviction in the idea itself, so much so that I was embarrassed to even talk about it. In essence I was the world's greatest marshmallow, no joke.

How did I get out of this place? How do I continue to grow and develop to reach my own potential?

In one word: modeling.

How I Stopped Kissing And Became An Entrepreneur

My introduction to modeling was not glamorous or anything special and, to my upset, I wasn't born with this skill. I was asked, as part of training program, to study some form of excellence, to look at a set of results I would like to create in my life and then find someone who I could model this from. This was a stumbling block, a self confessed ex-perfectionist I continued to spend the next four weeks dreaming (procrastinating) about what I might 'model.'

Being only seventeen and having teenage hormones running around my body 24/7, I spent the whole time thinking about how I was going to model elegant and tantalizing kissing! I thought this would be the perfect chat up line and excuse to find five gorgeous female volunteers and conduct 'extensive research.' I was so serious about it I was fierce. Unfortunately, my course tutor and me weren't on the same page. I later found out this was because he had already written a similar paper on this, three years prior. Oh well.

So, this left me another option. I would set about studying what made entrepreneurs tick. Specifically, how to identify unmet market needs and evaluate business opportunities. This seemed most appealing, sexy and just damn cool to me. At the time it seemed so mysterious I considered it a dark art. In short, I wanted to learn what made money and what didn't.

Enter Tom Charnock, a sixty something serial entrepreneur who agreed to meet with me for what was planned to be only one hour. Eight hours later, he was driving me home, a trait I would quickly learn he is well known for; I call it generosity. Tom and I had meet only on one occasion, prior; it was a real chance meeting in a lobby. A colleague and best friend told me some of what he had achieved.

So, what qualified Tom as a model?

His previously track record would a fill a book and even to this day I am still finding out some of the amazing things he has done.

Here's just a handful:

O   Bluebird Toys started in the 1980's recession within twenty years had revenue of £40 million. He had created and succeeded in setting up a business when, at the time, so few would have attempted to. This is something to me that instantly set aside Tom from other entrepreneurs.

O   He has been involved in the acquisition of over seven companies and publicly floated Bluebird, which was eventually sold to Mattel Toys.

O   He had been involved with some of the world most successful products.

O   He had some serious weight in turning around failing business in the shipyard industry.

O   He is master communicator, extremely intelligent, a real charmer and someone I want to spend time with (Note: I never pick a model that I don't like as a person. It is your decision, but I want to spend time with people who I enjoy being with, above all else – this is one of my highest values).

From Sled Dog Musher's to Comedians -
How To Harness Their Success & Make It Yours
I look at modeling in two forms, conscious and unconscious, and both are of great value. My primary goal is in being around any mentor or model as much time as possible, in their environment. I recognize that my unconscious mind will absorb so much in just being around them and listening to them. So very often I will detach myself from the result and let it do its job.

I have been honing the following strategy after recently modeling serial entrepreneur, experienced CEO and author Rikki Hunt. Rikki's experience is nothing short of mind blowing; he has driven up turnovers in companies operating in the retail and technology space of up £1.2 billion, consistently delivers success to the tune of multi-millions in whatever he turns his hand to and was the youngest ever MD of a British Petroleum company.

What I love about Rikki is his humility; there is no huge ego with this guy at all. He is generous with his time and does not hesitate to help out where he can, I have hugely valued his advice and I am always hungry for more. Rikki is always respectful to me and his latest venture, Digital City, is a company that inspires me and I want to see succeed.

Lessons from a Boa Constrictor
Snakes grow to the size of their cage, and I have adopted this philosophy in my own life, extensively. Today I am of the mindset that if I am not growing within my peer group, I am not growing at all. Which is not strictly true but it keeps me honest and focused on developing these important relationships. So, what's next for me? I have dangerously big and outrageously ambitious targets, backed up by a strong sense of belief that within the next ten years I will be modeling bestselling author and entrepreneur Timothy Ferriss, illusionist Derren Brown, Keysi fighting method founder Andy Norman, parkour and stunt man Chase Armitage, base jumpers in Japan, among many other fantastic souls who I am yet to meet.

Maybe I will be modeling readers of this book one day, who knows! The best part is I can pick and mix whatever skill and the person I want to learn it from. What will you model?

My models' social recognition, celebrity and societies definition of "success" is of no importance to me. What has value to me is their Jedi like mind skills and elegant strategies they possess and I consequently want to develop. Dream and dream big and remember that as we are all students and teachers, as you have something to learn from other people, you also have something to teach them.

How To Recruit Your Own Model
(With The Plan to Become An Ubermentor)
At the risk of exposing my strategy to my models, I want to give you the opportunity to find how you can recruit and develop a meaningful and reciprocal relationship with your very own ubermentor.

ACTION STEP # 1:
Call at least one mentor each day for at least five days.

It is always preferable, whenever possible, to meet your mentor face to face. Where would you be most likely to come into contact with your mentor? That's the place you need to hang out!

When you are looking to meet a mentor, they need to feel they have rapport with you, you have established trust and when you add value to their life (which we will cover later on) their boundaries around time in relation to you will shift. So, how do you get to this stage? Simple, find someone who you know or could get to know well who is ideally a raving fan of yours, who will sell you into your target.

When contacting mentors email should not become a crux. Only email after attempting to call at least twice or when geographic boundaries are a show stopper. To get the best results on the phone, I would suggest you call before 9:00 am and after 5:30 pm; this is to reduce the likelihood of your call getting caught up in "traffic" when everyone else is calling during typical business hours.

ACTION STEP # 2:

Identify one question you are not able to answer yourself by any other means i.e. Google, books, an Expert etc.

My personal favorite is to find material published by my target mentor or any other literature; interviews, documents, profiles, websites - the list goes on. Your goal is to have a particular and specific question that you cannot answer by yourself and, by inference, only they can answer. When this is in reference to an article, book, philosophy, idea or approach, you get twice as many gold stars. Chances of success are high. Online there should be something if not anything that is in reference to your mentor that you can ask. Social media is here to help, so use it! And, always, always, always state clearly what you have done to help yourself when asking others for help. Always!

ACTION STEP # 3:

Ask yourself, if I was guaranteed to succeed and not to fail who would I ask to mentor me? Bestselling authors? Celebrities? Ultra-successful CEOs?

Write a list and get creative. The best place to look for contact details is your mentors office, PR Agent or publishers. In the past I have had great success when connecting through Facebook, which is not to be shunned. When I encourage people to undertake this practice I notice people overestimate the difficulty of getting a phone number and, therefore, take no action.

What you do next depends on how the conversation goes. If the conversation lends itself to it, I would create a strong reason to come back to your mentor with another excellent and unanswerable question.

If you are going to take immediate action on the advice you have been given (and I would highly recommend it) ask your mentor permission if you can come back to them and let them know how you got on. Alternatively, does he/she bring something up in conversation that would give you a valid reason to contact them again?

What's important, here, is that you make an investment in your relationship. So, initially build rapport, build rapport, build rapport. Without value you cannot develop your relationship.

My favorite close to a conversation is, "Would be it OK if very occasionally, from time to time and I had a really tough question I can't answer, I could keep in touch via email?" People don't like to say no to it. I love it because it leaves the door open to future conversations, that is your end goal.

Rules of The Game:
How To Literally Double Your Response Rate - Every time.
Ever played golf? Or at least watched it on TV? Well contacting people with the intention of enrolling them in what you are doing has an etiquette that is likened to golf. Here's the good stuff I have learnt through painful mistakes.

Now I want to share it with you.

O   Be concise, short and clear in what you want. This makes things easier for everyone. If you can't show respect for a person's time now, you won't when they are giving precious hours to cover issues you really need their help with.

o Never have "small change" conversations. Small change is meaningless small talk to either avoid something or to be building rapport.

o If you have met recently or know someone they are good friends with - name drop. This gives people permission to trust you. Get it in early to the conversation without being obvious or out of place.

o A classic sales trick (you're selling yourself here, whether you aware of it or not) is to tell stories rather than facts. If you need to convey information, don't list it off aimlessly; you need to be building rapport by taking them on a journey. How did you get to where you are now? Remember my advice early on and keep it concise.

o Give him/her an option. Ironically, when you give busy people (which they are most likely to be) the option to decline your olive branch, this will get a better response rate than not doing so. Why? People love to feel they have choice and that they can exercise it.

One Life Stand

I would encourage you to ask yourself when meeting your model, how am I developing this relationship? If you are serious and committed to getting the results, you won't want this to be a fling. You need to develop a practice of constantly giving value.

What I have come to learn is people love to help. Models feel significant, important, valued, helpful and very often get a sense of connection when sharing their skills with others. Any time you facilitate the opportunity for your model to experience these emotions, you are adding value. Although it may feel like you are not adding a whole lot of value to their lives, in reality your adding more value than you will ever know.

Experience has shown me that there is one consistent way in which models or mentors wish to receive repayment: your ability to apply the information they have provided. For a moment get into their shoes. Would you feel as motivated to give someone your energy and time if you knew they weren't making any attempt to use it? Conversely, can you imagine how it feels for your mentor to watch you grow? What will they get in return when you succeed? Exposure? Credibility? Other opportunities? Satisfaction? Pride? The list is long, as you will discover when you start this process.

So in conclusion, get out there and find your own personal Yoda and do it Today.

Me again

A big thank you to Glenn for taking the time to share with us his strategies for modeling and how he has applied them in his life. I appreciate that Glenn's style of doing thing might not be yours; it does work, though, so I encourage you to take his methods, make them yours and get great results, like Glenn did. Having the right mentors in life can make such a huge difference to achieving your goals; both you and they will benefit enormously from the relationship. Remember, though – you are not aiming for perfection and they have permission to be human too.

Getting the best from having a role model

So if, like Glenn, you want to really make the most of having a role model, you will want to know how to learn their skill as fast as possible and do it as well as they do. Whilst you could have roles models that are famous, celebrities, historic characters and heroes and even fictitious characters, it is much more effective if you have a role model who is both real and accessible to you.

Do as Glenn did, ask permission to spend time with them to both observe what they do and to ask them questions. Get to know them and to know how they think, feel and do what they do. Below are some questions you will find useful to ask your role model, take a copy of them with you.

Beliefs

O Ask your chosen role model what makes it worth doing the skill that they have? What motivates them to do it?

O Ask them what else do they believe about this skill? For example do they believe it's is it easy, or it's hard, or it's fun, or it's boring, etc.

O How do they react to failure?

O How do they know when they are being successful?

O Make a note of any beliefs that they have that are different to your beliefs about that skill.

O Imagine what it would be like for you if you had their beliefs about the skill. Look for the difference that these new beliefs make. If they make a useful difference, keep them. If not, throw them away.

Emotions

O Ask them to think of a time they did the skill that you want to learn.

O As they go back to the time when they did that skill ask them what emotions were they feeling at that time?

O Are there times when they do that skill that they have different feelings?

O   If they have different feelings at times, ask them which were the most useful emotions to feel and how did they change their emotions when needed to do the skill?

O   In your imagination, try these qualities and emotions out for yourself as you imagine doing the skill.

What are they thinking?

O   Ask your role model to remember a time when they used this skill and, as they remember doing it, ask what is the first thing they are aware of. Did they picture something in their mind? Say something to themselves? Or have a certain feeling about it?

O   Make a note of what they tell you.

O   In your imagination have a go for yourself, using what they just told you.

O   Ask them how they know they have finished doing the skill. Ask for the last thing they are aware of. Is it images, sounds or feelings? Try this on in your imagination. If in doubt, ask them for more information.

External Behavior

O   Be curious and ask what goals do they set?

O   Find out from them how do they know they are achieving their goals?

O   Ask them what do they do, specifically, to achieve these goals, and what do they do when that doesn't work, i.e. what's plan B?

Practice

o   In your imagination, rehearse all of the steps with their beliefs, emotions and thoughts until you have mastered the skill.

o   Oh...And have fun doing it!!

What would you love to do better?

So go on then, think for yourself what would you love to be able to do better? It could be a skill, a quality you admire in someone or a behavior. For example, would you like to be more enthusiastic or passionate about something? Would you like to be able to juggle? Would you like to be more curious about things around you? Would you like to be fitter or healthier in some way?

Make a list in the space below.

For each of the things you identified above, write down who you know that does those things really, really well and makes them look easy, or does these things elegantly and effortlessly?

Take one at a time. Contact your role model and ask them the questions that we just went through. Try on their beliefs, emotions and thoughts to accelerate your learning and have fun!

Being a role model

As you grow into who you are, you will undoubtedly become a role model for others. You might know that you are and you might not; sometimes you are not aware of the people around you who admire you. What a compliment that is, though, that others look up to and recognize your gifts and strengths and want to emulate them for themselves.

Attempting to be the perfect role model will do both yourself and the person who looks up to you a disservice. a) It puts unnecessary pressure on you and b) It gives the other person unrealistic expectations of themselves, too. I had a lady who came on one of my courses who made the mistake of trying to be the perfect role model for the staff in the nursing home that she managed. She finally realized that instead of respecting her for being so precise at everything, they were intimidated by her, which was not what she had intended.

"So, permission to be human when being a role model, too."

It's OK to get things wrong and not have to hide it!
Not only is it good to be human, it's OK to make mistakes and not feel that you have to hide them. When you make a mistake and hide it or cover it up, it's a bit like telling a lie, pretending it never happened. You might think that you have got away with it, but your body knows differently and it affects your integrity.

As you hide the error an odd thing happens within you. You begin to feel uneasy and stressed because what if someone saw, or heard, or found out that you got it wrong? Little niggles and doubts and fears start to creep into your thoughts that affect how you feel and unconsciously will affect how you portray yourself to others. People start to notice, often at a gut level, that something isn't quite right and that you are not as congruent as before.

On the flip side, of course, if you admit that you're just human, too, the people that admire you will actually admire you that much more. Why? Because you were humble enough to admit you got it wrong. You were open enough to share the experience and you were generous enough to share the learning.

Give generously!
When things go wrong, not only do you get to have a learning experience, you get the gift of giving others the benefit of your learning, too. It's a blessing to know that other people make mistakes, too; it gives those around you permission to be human and both admit to and learn from their own short comings.

> "Accepting our mistakes is far harder than making them. If it weren't, the lessons wouldn't be of much value."

When you get it wrong it shows others that it's not the end of the world; it's simply an opportunity to do things a different way. It's a chance to set an example by taking responsibility for it whatever it was and taking care of it in an accountable way. What a way to lead the way!

One of the great benefits of modeling someone is that you get to learn from their mistakes and that means you not only save yourself the pain but you save yourself a lot of time, too! So when you share your lessons with others you get them to their goals so much faster. They will be very grateful for that and you get to celebrate their success with them, knowing that you played a little part in it.

Write down a time when something didn't go quite as planned for you. What have you learned from that and how could you share it with others so that they can benefit, too?

"Having a role model in life is a great thing to have; one who provides us with direction and inspiration.

However, we will forever be restricted by that person's limitations if we live within their boundaries.

Be influenced, but set your own standards and develop your own principles, if you are ever to live beyond someone else's dreams."

Jason Shahan

Chapter 8
<u>Allow Others to be Human, Too!</u>

The dangerous thing about perfectionists is that they attempt to project their perfection on to others. Excuse me? You're going to beat yourself up for not being perfect and then beat other people up for not being perfect, too? Let's consider that, shall we?

Set people up to win, not to be perfect

People will always rise to the level of expectation you have for them but in the case of perfection they can never win, because they can never attain the standard, so they end up feeling not good enough, less than, a failure. Do you really intend to make other people feel that way? I suspect not, so let's make sure you set others up to win, not to be perfect.

Use their gifts, don't dwell on weaknesses.

Before you give someone a task to complete, a project to work on or you simply ask a favor of them, have a think for a moment about what are their gifts? If the request you are making of them uses their talents then you can expect a high standard of return from them and they will most likely enjoy completing the request to a high standard.

If what you are asking of them is not what they would normally do, then you may need to consider the way in which you ask them to go about the task, using what they are good at. For example, invite them to use their creativity, or logic or organizational skills. They could perhaps complete the task including visual images ,or including lots of research, or consider it from a person-centered point of view.

If the other person has identified something that they would like to get better at and it's an opportunity to grow in a safe environment, it might be OK to ask them to do something that involves that skill and the feedback should be positive, constructive and supportive.

However, if what you are asking of them is really not what they are good at then you can expect disappointment, frustration and a feeling of not good enough from both you and them. The result can be very destructive and cause a loss of trust, respect and friendship.

I don't know about you but I like to allow people to feel good about themselves as often as possible, so that they can shine and develop what they are good at. I want people to feel rewarded and appreciated for the things they do well, so that they will want to do them again for themselves, for me and for others. I choose to look for what they did well and praise that, rather than look for the things that made it imperfect and criticize those things, leaving the person feeling bad.

My youngest daughter is a gymnast, a rhythmic gymnast to be exact, and she trains five days a week for a minimum of 4 hours each day. On the run up to an important competition, she and the other girls in the squad will put in many more hours than that, even taking time off school to train harder and longer.

The coaches at the club are very skilled and get fantastic results with the gymnasts that they choose to be in the squad. The methods that are employed by the coaches do not always have the best results, in terms of the morale and confidence of the girls they teach, though, which often brings them to my office to be coached in a different way, to increase their confidence and self belief, again.

There are many occasions when the girls feel like quitting because they are made to feel that they can't do anything right. They feel resentful of the fact that even though they did 98% of the routine better than they have ever done it before, all the coach can say is, "Your legs could be straighter," or "That throw needs to be higher," or "That arm is bent."

The standard for the coach is perfect and because the girls are not perfect they rarely get a well done, a "good job, today" or congratulations on doing so well, either in practice or even at a competition, where they have got through to the final and may even have won a medal. It breaks my heart when I see them cry because they are so disappointed after they gave their all and didn't even get an acknowledgement from the coach.

I understand that she just wants them to be the best but you have to acknowledge what they do well and build on that, not just continually point out their weaknesses. Give them permission to be human and allow them to feel good, then they are more likely to work on the other stuff to get your praise there, too.

Be clear about your expectations – People cannot mind read

One of the biggest challenges we face is unclear communication about the level of expectation we have of others. If we expect them to be perfect they have a right to understand that, so they can decline the responsibility and opportunity to fail!

Our standards are just that, our standards. Other people may have different standards, potentially not as high as the ones we set for ourselves and they need to know what it is we expect from them, otherwise they will complete the task to their standard and wonder why we are not happy with them.

Have you ever done something for someone and you did the best you could, you spent loads of time on it, getting it right, making it just so. You were really proud of your work. Then the other person came along and picked fault with it, pulled it apart and told you it just was not good enough? How did that feel for you? Not nice, right? And that's probably an understatement!

Perfect at work

There are times when you might feel the urge to expect someone to be perfect in their job and put unrealistic pressure on them, or criticize them harshly for being anything less than. For instance, do you find it unacceptable for any of the following people to be less than perfect 100% of the time?

Doctors	Leaders	Opticians	Models
Nurses	Spiritual	Parents	Sports men
Pharmacists	leaders	Teachers	Sports women
Politicians	Dentists	Actors	Your boss

And the list could go on. When they dare to show a slight weakness, a little flaw in their character, a chink in their armor, you are shocked. If they overlook something, you are up in arms. When they say something perhaps they shouldn't (in your opinion), you are taken aback. God forbid any of them should ever be tired, distracted, simply make a mistake!!

Is that really fair? Would you like to be under that constant pressure and scrutiny? I am and I hate it when people accuse me of being less than perfect! It's not my job to be perfect! My job is to be the best human being I can be and if I make a mistake I'll let you know that I'm human, too, that I'll apologize and take responsibility for my actions and put right, whatever it is.

Allow other people to be human, as long as they are conscientious, professional, caring and accept responsibility when things go a little pear shaped. The majority of the human race do not set out to make mistakes or cause deliberate harm, so cut them a little slack, occasionally.

Perfect at home

You spend your life looking for the ideal partner, you meet, you fall in love and then some how you change your expectation from ideal to perfect. Hmm…How does that work out for you?

Perfection has no softness, no forgiveness and no compromise. Imperfection is met with hard judgment and ouch! That hurts when you are on the receiving end. It's a recipe for the demise of a relationship. So if you want a long, lasting and fulfilling relationship – allow your partner to be human too.

The most damaging thing a perfectionist can do is to expect their children to be perfect. It drives those kids crazy! Sometimes quite literally! Those kids end up in therapy for years and/or on drugs, they are diagnosed with depression, anxiety, OCD, bi-polar disorder, social anxiety disorder…you name it – a label they can be given to prove it's not their fault they're not perfect – they have a disorder!

May be it's just the result of unrealistic expectations being forced upon them and they just needed a way to make you realize they are just human. Kids who grow up with parents who expect them to be perfect never feel good enough, worthy, loved and yet most parents actually are expecting perfection because they think it's best for their children. Ironic isn't it?

Step in to their shoes….

In order to set someone else up to win you first have to understand how they think, what they believe, what are their standards and how they view their world. They say you can never truly understand another until you have walked a mile in their shoes but how can you really ever actually do that?

If you have someone in your life either at home or at work who you have previously got frustrated with or annoyed by because they didn't meet your standards, they weren't perfect, then this exercise will really help you to step into their reality, so that you can re-think what you expect from them. It will also help you to know how to ask for what you need from them and give you an insight about how you might need to change your thoughts and communication, too.

Here's how. You might find this exercise easier to do with someone else guiding you through it. Alternatively, read through the instructions first of all. Do the first position, then read the next part and do the second position, then read the third part and do the next position, then read the fourth part and complete the exercise, i.e. take it one step at a time, reading in between each, rather than attempt to memorize it all!

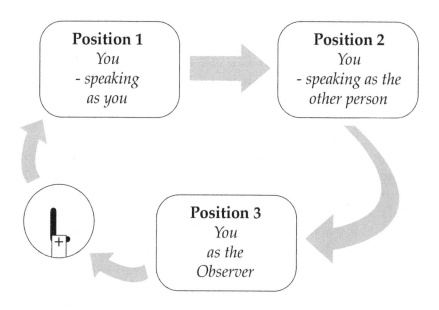

Part 1 – You as yourself

Imagine that you are standing at position one with the person that you have had a challenge with standing in front of you (position 2). As you see them standing there, tell them everything – what in your opinion has happened, how you feel about the situation and about them and why. Go on, permission to get it all out there, emotion and all, they can't defend themselves, answer you back or slap you from there!! Be as real as you possibly can and honest with yourself about the whole thing.

Did you get it all out? Once you have got the whole thing off your chest – go ahead and have a drink of water, shake off the emotion, get back to you again.

Part 2 – You get to be them

Now physically jump in to position 2 – the place where you had imagined them standing in front of you a moment ago and become them, the person you are having or have had the challenge with. Really get into character, their character by standing the way they would stand. Are they usually standing tall or slouched? Solid on two feet or with their weight on one side more than the other? Straight on or at an angle? What do they do with their hands or feet? How are they breathing? What expression would be on their face?

As you begin to speak in a moment, speak as they would. That means you need to use their tone of voice, at their speed and volume, using the words and phrases that they would use. With that combination of body language, voice and tonality, you now speak as if you were that person talking back to you. You can see yourself standing opposite you as you tell you how what you just heard makes you feel. As you become the other person, express what is going on for you as if you were thinking as them. State your view of the situation from their point of view, using their language, expressions and gestures.

When you have really given your side of the story from their perspective and you are sure it was from them, not from your reality of them, then you can step away and "shake them off" and be you again for a moment.

Part 3 – You are an independent observer

This position is very similar to an exercise you did earlier when you imagined the scene below you and you were looking down on it from an observer's point of view. Remember that?

You stand on a chair or imagine the two people in the conversation (you and the other person) nice and small below you. Look down onto the scene and take in just what is happening between the two characters as if you were a fly on the wall, or as if you were a reporter from a newspaper, asked to go and get an overview, so that you can write an article about it.

As you take in all aspects of the situation and the differing points of view, notice what is going on there. Where are the common goals? Where are the barriers? Who needs to do what to resolve the challenge? Stay objective – you are not part of the scene of the story, you're just looking in on strangers.

When you have noticed all of the things you need to be aware of, step off the chair safely, or step back away from the scene if you were just imagining them small below you from the floor, and "shake off the reporter."

Part 4 – What did you learn?

Step in to the Learning Zone – that little spot on the floor between position 3 and where you were you at the start of the exercise (position 1) and ask yourself the following questions. Write down the answers either below or on a separate piece of paper:

1. What did I learn from this exercise?

2. What did I learn about the other person's reality of the situation?

3. What did I learn about my part in the challenge?

4. How do I need to change my approach with this person?

5. When I next have a conversation with this person, how will I now address the challenge differently, using what I have learned?

You do not have to agree with the way someone else looks at the world or the challenge, but appreciating how they see things, to understand why they act in a certain way, is well worth the time invested when you come to have a conversation or negotiation with them in the future; they will be so impressed that you took the time and effort to really consider their thoughts, feelings and issues.

Support them, don't judge them

It is the easiest thing in the world to do – to make assumptions and pass judgment on people who do not meet your exacting standards, who do not make the grade as perfect. As you make the judgment that that person is not good enough because they failed the perfect test, do you start to actively look then for other evidence of imperfection in them?

O   He didn't say good morning to me – he's so rude!

O   She didn't offer me a drink – she's so selfish

O   He got home from work last night and just sat in front of the TV – he's so lazy

O   She is always putting more lipstick on – she's so conceited

O   He's always fooling around – he's so shallow

O   She threw that whole pack away just because she didn't like it – she's so wasteful

And on, and on, and we could go on for ages with so many more examples. As you look for their faults does that make you more perfect? Or does it in some way allow you to feel better about yourself? I was just wondering why we do that. Looking for evidence to support the imperfection rather than looking for the positive intention of the person in the action. Maybe the assumption made in the judgment is incorrect and there is a different reason for the behavior.

Andrew was a young man who came on a youth course with us. He was sixteen years old, had just left school and had been fortunate enough to find a job doing some manual work. He didn't enjoy it but it was a job and gave him a little bit of an income and independence.

Andrew was the most disruptive delegate in the room on that course, constantly talking loudly, inappropriately, attention seeking. He wasn't listening to the trainer or the other delegates because he was thinking about how he could be in the spotlight next. He persistently interrupted with comments about going to the pub and how much he drank and how much he wanted a drink.

His diet was appalling and consisted mainly of sugar, fizzy drinks and caffeine, oh, and beer, according to Andrew. He was, not surprisingly, unfit, overweight, had a poor complexion and was lethargic much of the time.

His behavior was not only challenging for the leaders of the course, it was annoying to the other delegates, so much so that by the afternoon of day one they physically segregated themselves from him by moving their chairs well away from his so that he was sitting alone.

I am pretty sure that by now you have made some assumptions or judgments about Andrew. Perhaps you think that he is lacking in social skills or that he is rude and arrogant. May be you have decided that he is uneducated and only thinks about himself. He just likes to be the centre of attention all the time.

I wonder whether you would have got fed up of his behavior quickly and challenged him about it. You would have been forgiven for asking him to be quiet and keep his comments to himself. You might even have considered asking him to leave as he was causing so much disruption. In your judgment you could easily have dismissed him as a no hoper, many others already had and he knew that.

In their dismissal of Andrew those other people, his parents, friends, teachers, employer and fellow employees never got to see the incredible gifts, resources and strengths that Andrew has. His presenting behavior blinded them, preventing them from seeing beyond the façade and into his heart.

When I took the trouble to actually give him the attention that he so desperately needed, and I do mean needed not just wanted, I discovered that Andrew was just an amazing soul who had been given some really disempowering beliefs about himself, that he heard so often from others that he had turned them in to his truth and taken them on as his identity.

His parents had split up when he was young and he lived with his mum and stepfather, who treated him with disdain and was emotionally abusive to him. He still saw his real father but he had become an alcoholic and so was often in no fit state to appreciate his son's company. The emotional abuse and the lack of attention from his family took its toll on Andrew's confidence and self esteem, to the point that it was hard to find any at all.

He truly believed that there was nothing good about him and his lack of self worth put him at risk, because he truly didn't care what happened to him, whether he lived or died. He was not suicidal but he had no regard for his own safety. He so wanted to be accepted and loved that his drinking and talk of drinking was just his way of attempting be noticed by his father. To have something in common with him so that he could hang out with him and feel wanted.

If you have ever studied NLP you'll know that one of the many presuppositions of NLP is that people are not their behaviors. That is so true for Andrew. After receiving some positive attention and some tough love, in terms of dealing with his limiting beliefs, Andrew shows up in his life and the lives of others in a very different way now.

191

If you meet Andrew, today, you will meet a confident, caring and responsible young man who looks after his health much more proactively. You will be greeted with a big smile and compliments and an eagerness to help. He can tell you his strengths and gifts if you take the trouble to enquire and he is taking consistent steps towards reaching various goals that he has for his life.

One of Andrew's dreams was to be a landscape gardener and after the course he enrolled at Lackham College to do a course to learn the necessary skills. Lackham College was about a 24 mile journey from where Andrew lived and so he took the bus each day. He was so committed to completing the course that one day, when for some reason the bus was not running as usual, Andrew got on his bike and cycled the 24 miles there and back. He said to me, "All I kept thinking was that TeeJay said if you want something badly enough you'll find a way, so I did!"

Set people up to win and watch them excel beyond your expectations!

Is there someone in your life that at some time did not live up to your standards of perfection for some reason? Write below who that person was (or people if you are a serial perfectionist!) and how they fell short of perfect in your eyes.

What judgments and assumptions did you make about them?

What else could have really been going on?

How could you support them by setting them up to win instead?

Allow others to be Human in their Emotions

We have discussed how to set people up to win by setting high standards for them, within their capability and reality, in what we expect them to do or achieve and we also need to allow others to be human in their emotions, too.

In chapter 2 you discovered that, as humans, we are designed to feel the whole range of emotions and not think that we are supposed to just feel great all the time. The so called negative emotions come bearing gifts in the form of lessons, so go there, just don't live there – get the lesson, receive the blessing and move forward. That same applies to the people around you, also.

Remember that it is OK for them to feel the whole range of emotions, too; there are times when they will be feeling great and times when life happens for them and they feel not so great. Knowing what you now know about the lessons emotions give, you can better support them to get the gifts they need to move forward quickly.

There may well be times when you just don't understand why someone is feeling the way they do. Remember, their reality is their reality, created by whatever meaning they chose to give the event that happened and that determined the emotion that they are now feeling.

Here you have two choices:

1.   Support that person by helping them to find a more empowering meaning and/or to get the lesson

OR

Judge the heck out of them for feeling that way.

Just as before, with achievements and standards, when you judge someone you lose the ability to influence them and appreciate their gifts. The moment that person is judged by you, whether you realize it or not, they absolutely feel it and they will slam the door on you emotionally for it (and make their own judgments about you too)!

When I sat down to plan this chapter of the book an interesting thing happened as the Universe (or which ever higher power you believe in) delivered a very powerful lesson on the subject of judgment and how it feels to be judged.

I was in the middle of a particularly busy time in my business, in addition to that I had committed to writing this book and my personal assistant had just left the company to have a baby, so the admin tasks were temporarily back in my lap, too. I gave myself permission to be human and decided to ask someone who had been close to me for some help, that's something that I'm actually not good at, asking for help, so it was a big deal for me.

This particular friend had just last week offered to help out if I needed some support, so I naturally thought that the offer was genuine and I'd take them up on it. To my great surprise and disappointment I not only did not get the support I needed I also got a whole load of criticism, sarcasm, several lectures and massively judged.

At the time of asking for help I was already feeling under pressure, at a bit of a low ebb, energetically, and feeling a little vulnerable. The response that I got spiraled me out of my last bit of control and hope and plunged me head long into the depths of despair. It happened in a moment; as soon as I felt judged, logic went, emotions reacted and just hit rock bottom fast and hard!

I found myself questioning my whole life, my purpose and my truth. I actually felt broken in that moment, lost, ashamed and completely alone, like I have never felt before. I not only chose to kick him out of my life completely but to kick out any one else that I might have turned to for help in case they judged me, too. My defenses, all of the bricks in the wall that I had spent a long time taking down and being careful not to put back in, all went back up in a second!

I most certainly was given a very powerful and very painful lesson in what it is like to feel judged. Fortunately, I know that everything happens for a reason, a positive reason, and that good would come of that experience. I get to share it with you for starters! I gave myself time to feel the emotions, get the lessons and bounced back quickly from that terrible place. Oh, and took the defenses back down, too.

Judgment vs 'Love meant'
So having shared that with you, I highly recommend that instead of judgment you give the love that that person needs and deserves and really mean it. If you can remember in that moment that people are not their behaviors, that they are doing the best they can with the resources that they believe they have available to them at that time and give them love that is meant from your heart, you will most definitely get a very different response from them.

You will give them such a huge gift of kindness that they will appreciate so much. Rather than kick you out of their lives it will transform the relationship, whether the relationship is personal, intimate, friendship or business and take it to a new level. Rather than give them a criticism give them a big hug!

Hugs by the way are said to be good for you, they lower blood pressure and reduce the heart rate, they improve the mood and allow us feel accepted, valued and needed. What a brilliant gift to give someone who is feeling emotionally fragile in the moment; it will really give him or her a lift.

We all need hugs and we all need to feel that we can be heard. I think women especially in that regard. Sometimes when we are feeling emotional we don't want to be fixed, solved or have logic applied to the situation, we just want to talk! It's a lesson I learned from an amazing lady and relationship expert, Tammy Tantilla.

Tammy told me that women need to be heard, they have to tell their story and get it out. If they don't feel that the listener actually listened then they have to start again and tell it over. They need to keep restarting and re-telling until they finally believe the listener heard, so if you wonder why she keeps telling you the same thing over and over, perhaps it's a sign that you need to really listen!

Take people off Pedestals!

One thing that I have noticed about the role models that we have is that it is easy to be in awe of them. They are people that we admire so much that we almost hero worship them and put them on a pedestal. They can do no wrong in our eyes and we certainly would not want to do anything to upset them or risk being out of favor with them.

Let me let you in on a secret.

Having to live on a pedestal that someone else put you on is absolutely exhausting! Living up to your rose tinted expectations of them being perfect is hard work and they feel the pressure of that. Admire them, be inspired by them, learn from them and let them be human, too! Take them back down off the pedestal and give them a break.

Awe and Envy

Sometimes when you put others on a pedestal you are in awe of them and sometimes when you put someone on a pedestal it's easy to envy them, too. You wish you were them. They have everything you want, need and admire. Life must be so easy for them.

It's an odd thing but sometimes putting people on a pedestal actually can convert the awe in to envy and you can actually begin to resent them for being so perfect (in your eyes) so amazing, so successful, so beautiful, so...and so it goes on!

Not only are they feeling the pressure of living up to your perfect but now they are noticing and feeling your resentment of them building, too. It makes them feel nervous, uncomfortable and uneasy in your presence and they may begin to avoid you completely as a result. Not a good recipe for a modeling relationship!

Let's stop for a few minutes and consider this. Answer the following questions:

How does it make you feel when someone is in awe of you?

How do you feel when someone is envious of you?

Who in your life is putting you on a pedestal and how does that feel?

Who in your life are you putting on a pedestal right now?

If perfect is not possible, how are they human? List all of the things that remind you that they are human, too.

Finally, take them off the pedestal and have them on equal standing with you. You are both equal in your humanity and can live up to your own standards and expectations in your own ways.

**Share what you have learned -
about being human with others**

The biggest gift you can give others is to share with them what you've learned, here, about living, feeling and experiencing the gifts emotions give you. Let the people around you know that it's more than all right to be the best human being they can be: none of us are perfect and we don't expect them to be, either.

I trust that you will also remind yourself often too and do as I do... Catch yourself in that moment of attempting perfection... Smile to yourself and repeat the words...Permission to be Human. ☐

"Were I to await perfection,
my book would never be finished"
Chinese Proverb

ABOUT THE AUTHOR

TeeJay Dowe, founder of Momentum People, has helped hundreds of people to discover who they really are and what they really want from this life. Inspiring people to find the best within themselves, in order to give the best of themselves and giving people the opportunity to discover that we are all energy leaders in this life – you get to choose the energy that you affect and infect others with.

TeeJay graduated from Aston University with a degree in Pharmacy Bsc Hons and worked passionately in pharmacy for many years. She loved being able to help, support, encourage and motivate people and make a difference to how they felt. No wonder she progressed into the world of Coaching!! The two are really pretty similar aren't they! Getting people to take responsibility for their own lives and wellbeing, to set goals and to take action, to follow through consistently to make a difference to the quality of their lives.

TeeJay added to her pharmacy experience and qualifications to become a qualified coach in Business Performance and Life Coaching and has Diplomas in both areas. Trained as a Master Neurostrategist she is certified as a Master NLP Practitioner, Time Line™ Therapist and Master Hypnotherapist and as an NLP Trainer.

TeeJay is PASSIONATE about supporting people to uncover their gifts and purpose, empowering them to live an even more fulfilling life and specialises in supporting people to find their potential by growing their confidence and self- esteem.

TeeJay is a highly sought after speaker, trainer and international coach who absolutely walks her talk, goes there first and is not done yet!

For further information, downloads, workshops and details about coaching join me at www.perfectshun.com and follow me on twitter at @TeeJayDowe I would love to stay in touch, hear your thoughts, comments and continue to support you on your own Grand Adventure.

Love and Blessings

TeeJay